Sydney Higgins is a writer, educationalist and broadcaster. Born in Cornwall, he was awarded an M.Litt. by Bristol University for his dissertation on *The Staging of the Cornish Miracle Plays*. He has written over forty books for schools and his many radio programmes include a series, produced for the I.B.A., on the government of Great Britain. His biographies include *Rider Haggard: The Great Story-Teller* and *The Benn Inheritance*.

Anna Higgins is a graduate in American Literature of the University of East Anglia. She is a photographer and writer of many children's books, which have been translated into several European languages.

Both have travelled extensively throughout Europe, Africa and North America. They have three sons and homes in Suffolk and Italy.

To
NANCY & TONY BOOTH
who greatly helped with this trip

Acknowledgements

We are grateful for the help we received from the French Government Tourist Office in London, Relais & Châteaux, Châteaux et Demeures de Tradition, Château Accueil, La Castellerie, Châteaux Hôtels Indépendants, Les Etapes Francois Coeur, Relais du Silence, International Leading Association, Gîtes de France and Minotels France Accueil. Like anyone writing about châteaux, we also acknowledge our debt to the pioneer in the field, Philippe Couderc, author of *La Vie de Château*.

With only a couple of exceptions, we were well received by the proprietors or managers of all the châteaux we visited. We were most impressed by the kindness and consideration of the people we met, including those who spoke no English. We give them all our thanks.

Front Cover: Château de Boussac (59 in this guide).

Staying in the
Châteaux Hotels
of Eastern France

Syd and Anna Higgins

Roger Lascelles, Cartographic and Travel Publisher
47 York Road, Brentford, Middlesex TW8 OQP Telephone: 081-847 0935

Publication Data

Title	Staying in the Châteaux of Eastern France
Typeface	Phototypeset in Compugraphic Palacio
Photographs	Syd and Anna Higgins; the proprietors of châteaux.
Printing	Kelso Graphics, Kelso, Scotland.
ISBN	0 903909 83 9
Edition	First May 1990
Publisher	Roger Lascelles
	47 York Road, Brentford, Middlesex, TW8 0QP.
Copyright	Syd and Anna Higgins

Distribution

Africa:	South Africa —	Faradawn, Box 17161, Hillbrow 2038
Americas:	Canada —	International Travel Maps & Books, P.O. Box 2290, Vancouver BC V6B 3W5
	U.S.A. —	Boerum Hill Books, P.O. Box 286, Times Plaza Station, Brooklyn, NY 11217, (718-624-4000).
Asia:	India —	English Book Store, 17-L Connaught Circus/P.O. Box 328, New Delhi 110 001
	Singapore —	Graham Brash Pte Ltd., 36-C Prinsep St
Australasia:	Australia —	Rex Publications, 413 Pacific Highway, Artarmon NSW 2064. 428 3566
Europe:	Belgium —	Brussels - Peuples et Continents
	Germany —	Available through major booksellers with good foreign travel sections
	GB/Ireland —	Available through all booksellers with good foreign travel sections
	Italy —	Libreria dell'Automobile, Milano
	Netherlands —	Nilsson & Lamm BV, Weesp
	Denmark —	Copenhagen - Arnold Busck, G.E.C. Gad, Boghallen, G.E.C. Gad
	Finland —	Helsinki — Akateeminen Kirjakauppa
	Norway —	Oslo - Arne Gimnes/J.G. Tanum
	Sweden —	Stockholm/Esselte, Akademi Bokhandel, Fritzes, Hedengrens Gothenburg/Gumperts, Esselte Lund/Gleerupska
	Switzerland —	Basel/Bider: Berne/Atlas; Geneve/Artou; Lausanne/Artou: Zurich/Travel Bookshop

Contents

Introduction

What is a château? Is it a castle, a palace, a mansion, a stately home, a large country house, or a vineyard estate?

'Château' is a word used in France to describe all of these, as well as other less impressive buildings. A quick flick through this book will show the apparent infinite variety of places that are called châteaux. Of those that now exist, several were built in the eleventh century, while a couple are less than fifty years old. Some contain dozens of rooms, others only a few. There are châteaux in estates of several hundred acres; there are one or two that have only a small garden. The only generalisation that can be made about them all is that they have a stone or brick facade and almost always some form of fortification, even if it is purely decorative. Almost all are in the countryside and occupy sites that for centuries belonged to one or other of the French aristocratic families. Many châteaux either changed hands or were badly damaged during the French Revolution. With the Restoration, a large number of châteaux were either rebuilt or radically reconstructed.

So how did we make our selection? Our intention was that this guide-book should be as comprehensive as possible. We spent many months tracking down every place we could find that offered accommodation and was either called a château or looked like a château. Having completed our preliminary research, we discovered that there were over three hundred châteaux in France accepting paying guests. To cover them adequately, we decided to write two guide-books - one dealing with the châteaux in the western part of France and the other with those in the east. We then set off on several exciting tours of France, visiting, staying at and eating in an enormous variety of châteaux. The accommodation that is offered varies considerably in quality, quantity and price. Some of the places are family homes that accept a few paying guests for bed-and-breakfast. In these, the bedrooms may have changed little in the last hundred years - the furnishings are often precious antiques, the floors are highly polished oak boards, and the plumbing may well be archaic. There are also family-run châteaux that are, in everything but name, medium-sized hotels but, because officially they only accept paying guests and offer table d'hôte, they are considered to be private homes and thus avoid government regulations, inspection and price-controls. Other châteaux have been expensively converted into luxury hotels. Some of these successfully maintain the spirit and atmosphere of the ancient building, while others are as bland and anonymous as any other international hotel.

Inevitably, we have failed to discover every château, but of those we did encounter the only ones we have omitted from our guide are a couple of brand-new hotels which, without any justification, have been given the name 'château'. The rest are all included - the good, the average, the poor and the awful. Subject to the law of libel, we describe everywhere as we found it. Of course our view is subjective - what we hate, others may love. Of course we have prejudices - we dislike, for example, plastic flowers, reproduction furniture masquerading as genuine antiques, and all carpets, wallpaper and fabrics with a swirling pattern in garish colours.

Times are changing in rural France. Every month sees châteaux being opened to paying guests for the first time. In some cases it's because the owners are finding it difficult to maintain the old family home; in others a derelict house has been purchased and restored to make it into a hotel. Every year, some château-hôtels change hands; every year a few châteaux close for good. We shall endeavour to keep up-to-date with these changes, but for subsequent editions of this guide-book to be as accurate and useful as possible we need your help. Please send us your views and comments on any châteaux you visit, whether ones already in the guide or others that you feel ought to be included.

Using this Guide

The guide-book is divided into regions, where the châteaux are listed according to their department. All the regions in the east of France are covered, and arranged in order from north to south. At the end of the book there are several indexes, including alphabetical lists of the location and name of each château. There are other indexes of châteaux that have special facilities (such as swimming-pools) or are close to one of the autoroutes. A map giving the location of each château follows this introduction.

The heading
Many châteaux are in villages too small to have been allocated a postal number (or zip-code). When this is the case, the heading gives the location of the château in capitals, with the place used as the postal address in small type:
   e.g. TARGET - Chantelle
The heading also gives the region in capitals and the district in small type:
   e.g. AUVERGNE - Allier

The château
The name of the château is preceded by its reference number and followed by an identification of the type of accommodation offered:
   e.g. 59 CHATEAU DE BOUSSAC PG
The accommodation is graded:
   H = Hotel (subject to French Government regulations)
   PG = private home accepting Paying Guests

Our rating of the château
Two types of symbols are used:
     ♉ showing the degree of interior authenticity and
    ♉ ♉ the sense of château life
  ♉ ♉ ♉
     ★ showing the degree of modern comforts and the range
   ★ ★ of facilities
 ★ ★ ★

In addition, we have identified the following châteaux as having a special quality or excellence:

- ❦ 10 Hostellerie du Château ♙♙ ★ ★ ★
- ❦ 24 Château de Thoiry ♙♙♙ ★ ★
- ❦ 27 Château des Crayères ♙♙ ★ ★ ★
- ❦ 42 Château de Lesvault ♙ ★ ★
- ❦ 59 Château de Boussac ♙♙♙ ★ ★
- ❦ 61 Château de la Vigne ♙♙♙ ★
- ❦ 62 Château de Bassignac ♙♙♙ ★ ★
- ❦ 76 Le Château ♙♙ ★ ★ ★
- ❦ 100 Le Château Eza ♙ ★ ★ ★
- ❦ 102 Château du Domaine Saint-Martin ♙♙ ★ ★ ★
- ❦ 103 Mas de la Brune ♙♙♙ ★ ★
- ❦ 108 Château d'Entrecasteaux ♙♙♙ ★

Like the complete collection, the châteaux in our list of the current top-twelve are very varied. A couple are among the most expensive, while others have moderate prices; Entrecasteaux has only three guest-rooms, while Domaine Saint-Martin has twenty-five. Each, however, has extraordinary charm and appeal.

When open

It is not unusual for French hotels, especially those run by a well-known chef, to close for one day every week, except perhaps in high season. Many châteaux are cold, draughty places in winter and so sensibly they are then closed. A few château-hôtels near Paris are not open in August.

Prices of rooms

The prices of rooms in hotels are fixed by the French Government and depend on the size, the bathroom facilities, the view and the furnishings. Proprietors accepting paying guests into their own homes can in theory charge what they like. There is no regulation on restaurant prices - and there is a tendency for them suddenly to increase during the high season. Rather than give the exact prices supplied by each of the château, we have used in the guide letters to represent 200FF (or approximately 20 or 30):

A	1- 200FF	(up to 20 or 30)
B	201- 400FF	(up to 40 or 60)
C	401- 800FF	(up to 60 or 90)
D	601- 600FF	(up to 80 or 120)
E	801-1000FF	(up to 100 or 150)
F	1001-1200FF	(up to 120 or 180) etc.

So, for example,

Total number of rooms: 28 C-F

means that the prices of the 28 rooms are between 401FF and 1200FF. Unless otherwise stated, the costs are for a double room for one night.

In many places it is possible, on payment of a small surcharge, to have an extra bed in a room for a child. In most hotels, what is called a suite is really two connected bedrooms with a common bathroom. Some of the more expensive châteaux do have suites that consist of a bedroom and a lounge. In this guide, if a châteaux is shown as having an apartment, it will be a group of rooms including a kitchenette that can usually be rented only by the week.

Breakfast is provided by all châteaux, including those without a restaurant. In a few cases - all noted in the details of the château - breakfast is included in the cost of accommodation. Elsewhere, proprietors usually assume that guests will purchase breakfast, but be warned - the cost and what is provided vary considerably. In some places, breakfast is a rip-off. It is extremely galling to be charged 50FF for a luke-warm coffee and a stale croissant. So, in all but first-class hotels, check the night before what is provided for breakfast and, if you don't think it's likely to be good value, say you don't want it. Few châteaux are very far away from a bar or a café where an excellent breakfast can be bought at a much more reasonable price.

In châteaux where there is a restaurant, it is usually possible to have demi-pension (and three or four places accept guests only on this basis). Often a minimum length of stay is demanded. The charge shown for demi-pension is per person, although it is normally available only to a couple sharing a room.

Credit cards
Although most hotels accept some credit cards, few accept them all and many are reluctant to take any. Few private homes will accept credit cards. If in doubt, check first.

Tips
In the hotels and restaurants of France, unlike most of those in the United States and some in the United Kingdom, it is usual for a 10 or 15 service charge to be added to (or included in) the cost of a meal.

We do not approve of this practice, especially as there's no guarantee that the additional charge is distributed among the members of staff who are actually providing the service. The argument usually presented in favour of service charges is that they prevent customers and waiters from being embarrassed by tipping. It does no such thing because, at least in first-class hotels, tips are still expected, in addition to the iniquitous catch-all service charge.

When we discussed the matter of tipping with the managers of several first-class or luxury hotels, all stated that their staff expect tips and that the minimum amounts paid by customers satisfied with the service are:
● for the waiter (lunch or dinner) - 30FF, left at the table
● for baggage delivered to or collected from the room - 10FF
● for the rest of the staff - 50FF, on paying the final bill.

In hotels that are not classified as 'luxury', it is assumed that tips will be given only for additional or special services, which unfortunately includes, if you're lucky enough to find anyone willing to do it, the carrying of baggage to the bedroom.

However, unless you've really been impressed by the service or have money to burn, we recommend parsimony.

We also suggest that it's sensible to check all bills. On two occasions during our tour of the chateaux in this guide, we discovered that we'd been overcharged!

Directions
We wasted many hours driving around in search of well-hidden châteaux throughout France. Even the directions given by the owners were usually inadequate. We have tried to give detailed directions for all entries in this guide, usually from the nearest large town.

Reservations

Of course, it is possible to drive up to a château and ask if a room is available. At many times in the year, you'll certainly find something, although it may cost more than you had expected to pay. But it isn't an advisable thing to do. Many châteaux are miles off the beaten track and, like hotels throughout France, most of them will not have spare rooms in July and August. If your journey is well planned, by all means write. If a room is booked sufficiently far in advance, a deposit will be required. Having written at least once to all the châteaux in this book, we have sadly to report that a small percentage of our letters did not arrive. We found that the most satisfactory way of making a reservation was by telephone. It costs very little and an answer is immediately obtained. You will be asked to give your expected time of arrival. If, for any reason, you find that you're going to be late, ring the château, otherwise you may find that your reservation has been cancelled.

It is often easier to find a hotel room than it is a table at a restaurant. Even for a place with a modest reputation, it is advisable to make a reservation. At the best restaurants, it may be necessary to book weeks in advance. But it's always worth telephoning to find out. Cancellations do occur. The most difficult time is Sunday lunch, when many French families set off for gastronomic outings to the countryside and fixed-priced tourist menus totally disappear.

Driving in France

Many guide-books contain pages of advice and instruction for foreign motorists travelling in France. We'll keep ours simple.

Take your time. France is a huge and fascinating country. Enjoy it. Never overestimate the distance you can travel in a day.

Use the country roads. Even during the high season, it is possible to drive in France along almost deserted, but adequate minor roads that pass through delightful countryside. To reach many of the châteaux in this book, you have no alternative but to choose the roads less travelled by.

Fill up with petrol when you have the opportunity. Off the autoroutes, garages, like shops, are liable to close for long lunchtimes, some part of the weekend, and on public holidays.

Have a good road map open in the car. In rural areas of France it is not unusual to find stretches of road completely closed because of road-repairs, cycle-races, accidents, film-making or religious festivals. Diversion signs are not always reliable. If you're unsure of where to go, stop and refer to your map.

Let them overtake. Everybody driving in France will have come across the lunatic who seems desperate to establish contact between the bumper of his vehicle and the exhaust-pipe of yours. Periodically, and usually just before a blind-bend or when a stream of traffic is approaching, this king-of-the-road will try to overtake. The only sensible way to deal with such people is to pull over as soon as possible and let them pass.

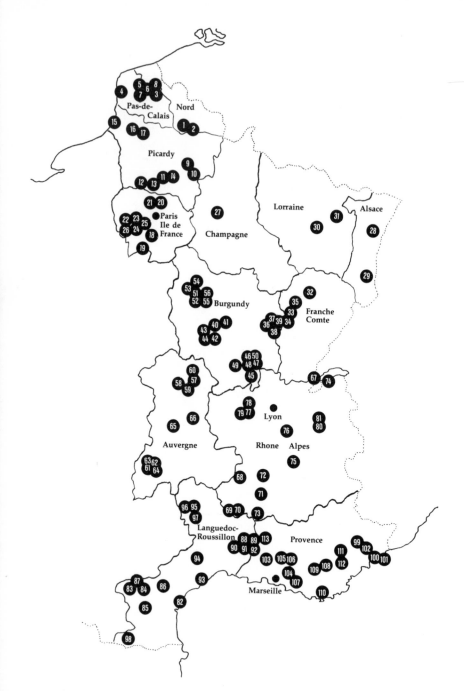

The Châteaux of Eastern France. The numbers on the above map refer to châteaux described in this guide.

List of Châteaux

Yvelines
22 Rolleboise, Château de la Corniche
23 Saint-Germain-en-Laye, Pavillon Henry IV
24 Thoiry-en-Yvelines, Château de Thoiry
25 Villepreux, Château de Villepreux
26 Villiers-le-Mahieu, Château de Villiers-le-Mahieu

CHAMPAGNE

Marne
27 Reims, Château des Crayères

ALSACE

Bas-Rhin
28 Barembach, Château de Barembach
Haut-Rhin
29 Rouffach, Château d'Isenbourg

LORRAINE

Meurthe-et-Moselle
30 Rehainviller, Château d'Adomenil
Moselle
31 Tarquimpol, Château d'Alteville

FRANCHE COMTE

Haute-Saône
32 Epenoux, Château d'Epenoux
33 Malans, Château de Malans
34 Nantilly, Château de Nantilly
35 Rigny, Château de Rigny

BURGUNDY

Côte-d'Or
36 Gilly-les-Cîteaux, Château de Gilly
37 Longecourt-en-Plaine, Château de Longecourt
38 Nuits-Saint-Georges, Hôtel Château de la Berchère
39 Saulon-la-Rue, Château de Saulon-la-Rue
Nièvre
40 Guipy, Château de Chanteloup
41 Lantilly, Château de Lantilly
42 Onlay, Château de Lesvault
43 Pouges-les-Eaux, Château de Mimont
44 Saint-Benin d'Azy, Manoir de Valotte
Saône-et-Loire
45 Ceron, Château La Fredière
46 Chagny, Hostellerie du Château de Bellecroix
47 Fleurville, Château de Fleurville
48 Ige, Château d'Ige
49 Saint-Aubin-en-Charollais, Château de Poujux
50 Saint-Germain-du-Plain, Château de Saint-Germain-du-Plain

Yonne
- 51 Auxerre, Le Parc des Maréchaux
- 52 Mailly Le Château, Le Castel
- 53 Prunoy, Château de Prunoy
- 54 Savigny-sur-Clairis, Hostellerie du Château de Clairis
- 55 Vault-de-Lugny, Château de Vault-de-Lugny
- 56 Villeneuve-la-Dondagre, Castel Boname

AUVERGNE

Allier
- 57 Bressolles, Château de Lys
- 58 Parc Saint-Jean, Château Saint-Jean
- 59 Target, Château de Boussac
- 60 Villeneuve-sur-Allier, Château du Riau

Cantal
- 61 Ally, Château de la Vigne
- 62 Bassignac, Château de Bassignac
- 63 Champagnac, Château Le Lavendès
- 64 Salers, Château de La Bastide

Puy-de-Dôme
- 65 Bort-l'Etang, Château de Codignat
- 66 Chaptuzat, Château La Roche

RHONE ALPES

Ain
- 67 Divonne-les-Bains, Château de Divonne

Ardèche
- 68 Lamastre, Château d'Urbilhac
- 69 Les Vans, Château Le Scipionnet
- 70 Sampzon, Hostellerie du Château de Sampzon

Drôme
- 71 Etoile-sur-Rhône, Château de Clavel
- 72 Montboucher-sur-Jabron, Château de Montboucher
- 73 Rochegude, Château de Rochegude

Haute-Savoie
- 74 Sciez, Château de Coudrée

Isère
- 75 Eybens, Château de la Commanderie
- 76 Faverges-de-la-Tour, Le Château

Rhone
- 77 Jarnioux, Château de Bois Franc
- 78 Saint-Jean-d'Ardières, Château de Pizay
- 79 Villefranche-sur-Saône, Château de Chervinges

Savoie
- 80 Le Bourget-du-Lac, Château-hôtel L'Orée du Lac
- 81 Ruffieux, Château de Collonges

Aude
- 82 Bages, Domaine d'Estarac
- 83 Belflou, Château de la Barthe
- 84 Carcassonne, Domaine d'Auriac
- 85 Couiza, Château des Ducs de Joyeuse
- 86 Peyriac-Minervois, Château de Violet
- 87 Villemagne, Castel de Villemagne

Gard
- 88 Arpaillargues, Château d'Arpaillargues
- 89 Bagnols-sur-Cèze, Château de Coulorgues
- 90 Ribaute-les-Tavernes, Château de Ribaute
- 91 Roquemaure, Château des Cubières
- 92 Saint-Laurent-des-Arbres, Château Beaupré

Hérault
- 93 Caillan, Château de Caillan
- 94 Madières, Château de Madières

Lozère
- 95 La Malène, Château de la Caze
- 96 La Malène, Château de la Malène
- 97 Meyrueis, Château d'Ayres

Pyrénées-Orientales
- 98 Molitg-les-Bains, Château de Riell

PROVENCE

Alpes-Maritimes
- 99 Cipières, Château de Cipières
- 100 Eze, Le Château Eza
- 101 Eze, Château de la Chèvre d'Or
- 102 Vence, Château du Domaine Saint-Martin

Bouch es-du-Rhône
- 103 Eygalières, Mas de la Brune
- 104 Meyrargues, Château de Meyrargues
- 105 Saint-Rémy-de-Provence, Château des Alpilles
- 106 Saint-Rémy-de-Provence, Château de Roussan
- 107 Salon, Abbaye de Sainte Croix

Var
- 108 Entrecasteaux, Château d'Entrecasteaux
- 109 Nans-les-Pins, Domaine de Châteauneuf
- 110 Saint-Cyr-sur-Mer, Château de Ferlande
- 111 Trigance, Château de Trigance
- 112 Vidauban, Château Les Lonnes

Vaucluse
- 113 Châteauneuf-du-Pape, Hostellerie Château des Fines Roches

1 CHATEAU DE LA MOTTE FENELON H

🛡🛡 ★ ★
Square du Château, 53400
  Cambrai, Nord
Tel: 27 83 61 38
Telex: 120 285 F
Propr: Hôtels & Residences
  du Roy
Direc: Mlle Elisabeth Brunet
Open: All year

Twin with bath   4 B-C
Double with bath   24 B
  Total rooms   28
(6 rooms in château - the
  rest in an annexe)

Restaurant: Closed Sunday
  evenings and evenings of
  public holidays.
Chef: M. Pascal Petit
Lunch: 1200 - 1330
Dinner: 1900 - 2130
Prix fixe: Menus at B
  A la carte available
Specialities: *Oeufs brouillés au
  caviar; Côte de boeuf en croûte
  de sel; Bar 'des Douves'.*

Lift. 22 ground floor rooms.

Seminars: max. 50
Groups: max. 20
Receptions: max. 250
Credit cards:
  American Express
  Diners Club
  Visa
English & German spoken

Tennis courts
Heated swimming pool

Châteaux Hôtels Indép.

In Cambrai. From Porte Notre Dame, take the road ahead, Avenue d'Albert 1er (which turns into Avenue de Valenciennes, the N30). After passing under the railway bridge, turn left on Allée Saint-Roch. It leads to the château. **Airport:** *Cambrai (5km)* **Station:** *Cambrai (1.5km)*

In 1850, the Brabant family, who were launderers in Cambrai, drained the large Lake of Escaudoeuvres so that they could use the land for bleaching. The task completed, Alphonse Brabant decided to build a house there, close to the factory. Château de Morenchies, as it was named, proved difficult to build. Because the land was marshy, the whole construction had to be built on piles of oak creating a vast grey-stone cellar beneath the white stone facade.

The château was attacked during the Prussian invasion of 1870. In 1918, it was bombarded by the Canadians and pillaged by the Germans, who built a concrete shelter in the cellars. During the Second World War, the Germans again occupied the building and looted the contents. As the house had been so badly damaged, it was not reoccupied after the war and was left to decay. The park with its beautiful views was soon overgrown.

In 1962 the estate was bought by the hotel-chain, Groupe Maison Familiale, with the intention of building a new hotel, but in 1973 it was decided to restore the château and the following year it was opened as Château de la Motte Fenélon, the name of an earlier owner, Francois de Salignac de La Motte Fenélon, the Archbishop of Cambrai. In 1986, the château was acquired by the hotel-chain, Hôtels & Residences du Roy.

After having driven past an industrial estate and several large blocks of flats, our hearts were sinking as we approached La Motte Fenélon. Nor did our first impressions improve matters. The château has a large bleak car-park and somewhat stark exterior. But our spirits rose as soon as we entered the building. The welcome was extremely warm and the atmosphere was most pleasant. Much of this was due to the director, Mlle Elisabeth Brunet, who throughout our stay impressed us enormously by her knowledge, skill and efficiency.

In the entrance hall, there is a suit of armour and several interesting antique pieces of furniture. Beyond, there is a delightful lounge with a chandelier, oriental carpets on a polished wooden floor and a gilded ceiling. On either side, there are two very elegant rooms. Breakfast is served in one that has a painted plaster frieze of fruit and elaborate bows and a splendid ceiling painted white and green. The other room is a wonderful salon with comfortable furniture. The walls are light and dark peach. There is an ornate painted ceiling and around the doors and mirror are elaborate plaster decorations. On the walls, there are attractive maple-framed flower illustrations.

Most of the bedrooms at La Motte Fenélon are in a motel-like annexe and must be paid for on arrival. Far superior are the bedrooms in the château, which although not grand have pleasant papered walls and are well furnished. The bathrooms are small but adequate. Because there are only six of these bedrooms, they usually have to be reserved some time in advance.

The cellar has been converted into a restaurant, called Les Douves, which provides good, moderately-priced food. There is also a grill in the converted stables.

The château is much used by the business community for seminars and receptions. It also provides a pleasant and comfortable place for tourists and travellers who want to stay and dine for a reasonable price on the outskirts of Cambrai.

2 CHATEAU DE LIGNY H

♥♥ ★ ★
4 Rue Pierre-Curie, 59191
Ligny-en-Cis-Haucourt,
Nord.
Tel: 27 85 25 84
Telex: 820 211 F
Propr: M. André Blot
Direc: M. & Mme Boulard
Open: 21 Feb - 7 Jan

No lift

Double with bath	4 C
Double with shower	2 C
Suites	3 E-F
Total rooms:	9

Specialities: *Foie gras de canard en terrine préparé au château; Caviar de Russie et son verre de Vodka; Noisettes d'agneau à la menthe poivrée.*

Swimming pool 5 km
Golf course 25 km

Châteaux Hôtels Indép.

13km south-east of Cambrai. From there, take the N43 towards le Cateau-Cambrésis. After 9km, at Beauvois-en-Cambrésis, turn right onto the D74. Follow the road to Ligny-en-Cambrésis-Haucourt. The château is in the village, up a small road on the left. **Airport:** *Cambrai (9km)* **Station:** *Cambrai (13km)*

In the mid-eighties, this small hotel was a member of Châteaux Hôtels de France and had a considerable reputation. It is no longer a part of that august organisation, but we are pleased to report that its standards, especially in the restaurant, are still high, the atmosphere is pleasing and the welcome is warm.

Although begun in the thirteenth century, the château as it now exists was largely built at the end of the seventeenth century. A tree-lined drive leads through the small park where fallow deer graze. The château has a round bell-tower with a six-sided pointed roof. There is also a Renaissance gate which crosses what was once the moat and leads into a pleasant courtyard with a central fountain.

The dining room is in the old armoury and has walls bedecked with hunting memorabilia, wooden rafters and a large open fire-place. Lunch and dinner are served by candlelight. There are several delightful dishes and an extensive wine-list. Furnished largely with antiques, the bedrooms are very comfortable. The expensive suites with their palatial bathrooms are luxurious. A peacful and romantic place.

3 L'HOSTELLERIE SAINT-HUBERT

H

🛡 ★★
1 Rue du Moulin, Hallines,
62570 Wizernes, Pas-de-
Calais.
Tel: 21 39 77 77
Proprs: M. & Mme Gérard
Delvar
Open: All year

Single with shower	1 B
Twin with bath	2 B
Double with bath	2 B
Total rooms:	5

No lift.

Restaurant: Closed Sun
evenings and Mon
Chef: M. Olivier Delvar
Lunch: 1200 - 1430
Dinner: 1930 - 2130
Prix fixe: Menus at A & B
A la carte available
Specialities: *Foie gras frais
de canard cuit au torchon;
Salade de langoustines et
ris de veau; Homard côtier
rôti aux aromates.*

Seminars: max. 25
Receptions: max. 130
Credit cards:
    Diners Club
    Eurocard
    Visa
English & Spanish spoken

Swimming pool
Tennis court
Golf course 5 km

9km south-west of Saint-Omer. From there, take the D928 towards Hesdin. After 7km, at Wizernes, turn right onto the D211 to Hallines. The château is down a road to the right in the village. **Airport:** *Lille (72km)* **Station:** *Saint-Omer (9km)*

From the middle of the fifteenth century, the waters of the River Aa, as they cascaded over a series of sluices, were used to power mills that made high quality paper. The industry reached its heyday during the nineteenth century. About 1800, a large château was built in a park on the bend of the river between two of the ancient mills. In 1890, the then millowners, the family Dambricourt, had the château remodelled in a style known as 'La Belle Epoque'.

During the twentieth century the paper-making industry in Hallines declined and by the outbreak of the Second World War production had ceased. Although still owned by the Dambricourt family, the mills and the château were abandoned. In 1987, Gérard Delvar, an expert in the making of glass-crystal, purchased the château, renamed it L'Hostellerie Saint-Hubert, and with the help of his wife and son, a qualified chef, turned it into a gastronomic restaurant and a small, extremely pleasant hotel. The quality of the food, the pleasant surroundings and standards of comfort have already received much well-deserved praise.

4 CHATEAU DE MONTREUIL H

★★

4 Chaussée des Capucins,
62170 Montreuil-sur-Mer,
Pas-de-Calais.
Tel: 21 81 53 04
Telex 135 205 F
Proprs. M. Christian & Mme
Lindsay Germain
Open: 1 Feb - 15 Dec

Twin with shower	2 B
Twin with bath	6 C
Double with bath	6 C
Total rooms:	14

(3 rooms in an annexe)
No lift. 3 ground-floor
rooms.

Restaurant: Closed Thur
  lunch, except in high
  season
Lunch: 1200 - 1400
Dinner: 1900 - 2130
Prix fixe: Menu at B
  A la carte available
Chef: M. Christian Germain
Specialities: *Fricasse de homard
cotier à la vapeur et estragon;
Turbot rôti aux aromates et
sauce porto; Soufflé aux
pommes et poires caramélisées.*

Demi-pension   C

Seminars: max. 25
Groups: max. 25
Receptions: max. 75
Credit cards:
  American Express
  Diners Club
  Visa
English, German &
  Spanish spoken

Tennis court 200m
Swimming pool 1 km
Golf course 12 km
Horse riding 15 km

Relais & Châteaux

*18km west of Le Touquet. From there, take the N39, which joins the N1 just before
Montreuil. Do not take the by-pass, but drive into the town. After passing through a tunnel
into the old town, the road swings right and then begins to loop back. At this point, turn
right into Rue des Bouchers. At the end, turn left into Chaussée des Capucins. The château
is on the left.* **Airport:** *Le Touquet (18km)* **Station:** *Montreuil (1km)*

Sadly, a fire caused considerable damage to this hotel in 1989. As a result,
substantial restoration and alterations have had to be undertaken.

Looking like a large Edwardian country house in southern England, the château
was built between the wars to a design by the English architect, Frank Wooster,
for the Fould-Springer family. After the Second World War, it became an hotel. It
was taken over in 1982 by Christian Germain, who was tutored by the famous
Roux brothers and was formerly the chef de cuisine at their Waterside Inn in Bray.
He runs the hotel with his English wife, Lindsay. His cuisine is first-class and has
rightly been awarded a Michelin rosette.

5 CHATEAU DE COCOVE H

★ ★

Recques-sur-Hem, 62890
  Tournehem, Pas-de-Calais.
Tel: 21 82 68 29
Telex: 810 985 F
Propr: Mme Annick Calonne
Open: All year

Twin with shower	4 B
Twin with bath	4 B
Double with shower	2 B
Double with bath	14 B-C
Total rooms:	24

Restaurant: Open every day
Chef: M. Alain Doriatti
Lunch: 1200 - 1400
Dinner: 1930 - 2130
Prixe fixe: Menus at A & B
  A la carte available
Specialities: *Cassolette de
ris de veau à la Perigourdine;
Blanc du turbot sabayon de
champagne.*

No lift. 10 ground-floor
rooms.

Seminars: max. 30
Groups: max. 40
Receptions: max. 70
Credit cards:
  American Express
  Diners Club
  Visa
English, German & Spanish
  spoken

'Swin' golf on site
Ponies and stables
Tennis courts 6km.

24km south-east of Calais. From there, take the N43 towards Saint-Omer. Just after passing over the A26, take the next left, the D217. Then, take the first left, which leads to Cocove. The château is on the left. **Airport:** *Calais (23km)* **Station:** *Saint-Omer (16km)*

Surrounded by peaceful countryside and yet only a couple of minutes' car-ride from the start/end of the A26, this eighteenth-century château was converted into a hotel in 1986. Much used by motorists using the Channel ports, it is comfortably-furnished throughout and has pleasant, modern bedrooms with well-equipped bathrooms. The restaurant overlooks the extensive grounds and its menus are reasonable in price and quality - although when we stayed the service lacked polish. A few facilities have been introduced - 'swin' golf, a jogging-track and a grill. The cellars have been converted into a well-stocked wine-shop. The hotel is part of the Best Western Mapotel group.

    The exterior of the château is very interesting. There is a long, three-storey central block with two small wings. In one of them, where the restaurant is situated, windows now enclose what was once an open, arched loggia.

    A pleasant enough place for an overnight stay.

---

6 HOTEL CHATEAU TILQUES H

🛡 ★ ★
Tilques, 62500 Saint-Omer,
 Pas-de-Calais.
Tel: 21 93 28 99
Props: European Country
 Hotels
Direc: M. Heinz Luchterhand
Open: All year

Twin with bath   47 C
Double with bath   6 C
 Total rooms   53
(24 rooms are in a new
 annex. A further 17 rooms
 are planned)

Restaurant: Open every day
Chef: M. Jean-Marc Arcangeli
Lunch: 1215 - 1400
Dinner: 1900 - 2200
Prix fixe: Menus at A
 A la carte available

No lift. 12 ground-floor
 rooms.

Seminars: max. 200
Groups: max. 100
Receptions: max. 200
Credit cards:
 Access
 American Express
 Diners Club
 Visa
English, German and
 Spanish spoken

Tennis courts

Inter. Leading Association

5km north-west of Saint-Omer. From there, take the N43 towards Calais. Shortly after entering Tilques, the château is along a well-signposted road to the right. **Airport:** *Lille (66km)* **Station:** *Saint-Omer (5km)*

Acquired at the beginning of 1989 by the British-based company that owns the Richmond Gate and Petersham hotels in London, this neo-Flemish château, which was built in 1891 and was previously known as 'Le Vert Mesnil', has been radically transformed. A new block has been built with 24 luxurious, pleasingly decorated modern bedrooms, each with their own terrace. In the old stables, a new restaurant has been constructed with traditional-style decorations and tapestry-covered high-back chairs. All the rooms in the château itself have been refurbished. The public rooms are very impressive. The entrance hall is most attractive with beautifully swagged blue curtains, comfortable chairs, a chandelier and arrangements of fresh flowers.

Providing, as it now does, such extensive reception and conference facilities, we expected Hôtel Château Tilques to be cold and anonymous. It wasn't. The atmosphere was very pleasant and we found the staff to be most helpful and welcoming.

7 LE MANOIR PG

♛ ♛ ★

16 Route de Licques,
  Bonningues-les-Ardres,
  62890 Tournehem-sur-
  le-Hem, Pas-de-Calais.
Tel: 21 82 69 05
Propr: Mme Christiane
Dupont
Open: All year

Twin with shower &wc. 1 B
Twin - shared bathroom 2 B
Double - shared bathroom 1 B
    Total rooms: 5

No lift

Table d'hôte on reservation
    A

No credit cards
English spoken

Fishing 500m
Tennis court 2km
Swimming pool 7km
Golf course 15km

Gîtes de France

28km from Calais. From there, take the N43 towards Saint-Omer. After 24km, at Nordasques, turn right on the D218 through Tournehem to Bonningues-les-Ardres. Le Manoir is on the right in the village. **Airport:** *Calais (29km)* **Station:** *Calais or Saint-Omer (21km)*

Many years ago, when Mme Dupont bought this house, the bill of sale called it 'Château de Bonningues', but she decided that it was too small for such a grand title and renamed it 'Le Manoir'. Built in 1840 in the style of Napoleon III, it is an attractive house of elegant proportions and pleasing detail. Surrounded by an enclosed garden of lawn and mature trees, it has a marvellous vista over rolling countryside. The interior has been little changed and so retains much of the atmosphere of the mid-nineteenth century. The ceilings are decorated with plaster coving and elaborate central roses; the floors are polished wood or tiles; and around the dining room walls there is an elaborate hand-painted frieze. The sitting room is cosy, with a large settee that has three white lace antimacassars on the back. China ornaments stand on every available surface. The bedrooms are cosy and quaint, with old furniture and high beds. The shared bathroom is immaculate. Particularly fascinating is the kitchen, with its old tiled walls on which hang pewter plates and a row of shining old copper saucepans. The ceiling is wooden and there is a pretty tiled fireplace. This is a charming house. Although having none of the grandeur of a château, its is an unspoilt example of nineteenth-century, French country-house architecture. The owner is a delightful hostess, who speaks only a little English. Close to Calais, Le Manoir is an ideal place to spend the first (or last) nights of a motoring holiday in an authentic French environment.

8 CHATEAU DE WAMIN PG

♛ ♛ ♛
Wamin, 62770 Le Parcq, Pas-
  de-Calais
Tel: 21 04 81 49
Propr: M. Bernard de Gouy
Open: All the year

Double with bath	1 A
Double with shared w.c.	1 A
(inc. breakfast)	
Total rooms:	2
No lift	

No restaurant
No credit cards
Swimming pool 4km
Tennis court 4km
Horse riding 4km
Gîtes de France

45km south of Saint-Omer. From there, take the D928 towards Hesdin. After 44km, and after the village of Le Fond-de-Barie, turn left on a narrow road to Wamin. Follow the long wall of the château and turn left towards the church. The château is on the left. **Station:** *Hesdin (7km)*

As you drive through the impressive gateway of Château de Wamin, there is the strongest impression of entering a place that is set apart from the real world, marooned in time. The whole estate appears to be encircled by a stone wall and beyond a vast circular lawn stands the magnificent château with its classical eighteenth-century facade, its shutters closed, and surrounded by silence. Inside is not disappointing. The side entrance leads into a dark hall with worn flagstones. Off this is a vast drawing room that can be used by visitors. (It was, by the way, the atmospheric location of scenes in *Le Soleil de Satan*, the French film that won the Palme d'Or at the 1987 Cannes Festival.) A marvellous wooden staircase leads upstairs, where there is an enormous long corridor with views over the wooded estate. Stuffed boars' heads hang on the walls. One of the guest bedrooms is huge and the other quite small. Both are delightful, although totally unpretentious. They have huge old beds on bare polished boards, with a few rugs and some old furniture. Breakfast can be taken either in the bedroom or en famille. The owner, M. Lefebvre de Gouy, is a farmer whose family has owned the château since 1811. He and his wife do not speak English, but are most kind and hospitable. Staying with them is a delightfully memorable experience. The surrounding countryside is extremely beautiful, including as it does the ancient Forest of Hesdin and the Valley of the Ternoise. Like Château de Wamin, the area is well worth discovering for yourself.

---

9 HOSTELLERIE LE GRIFFON H

25 Place General Leclerc,
  Blérancourt, 02300 Chauny,
  Aisne.
Tel: 23 39 60 11
Propr: M. Jacques Rousselet
Direc: Mme Paule Rousselet
Open: 15 Feb - 22 Dec

Twin with shower   7 A
Double with bath   9 B
Suite (max. 4)   1 B
  Total rooms   17

No lift. 4 ground-floor
  rooms.

Restaurant: Closed Sun
  evenings and Mon
Chef: M. Joel Menin
Lunch: 1200 - 1400
Dinner: 1900 - 1400
Prixe fixe: Menus at A
  A la carte available
Specialities: *Flamiche
  Griffon; Canard croisé à
  la compote d'oignon; Homard
  frais 'Vie en Rose'; Blanquette
  de langouste.*

Seminars: max. 45
Groups: max. 30
Receptions: max. 60
Credit cards:
  American Express
  Diners Club
  Visa
English & Italian spoken

Tennis court 5km
Swimming pool 5km

Châteaux Hôtels Indép.

42km north-east of Compiègne (exit 10 on the A1). From there, take the N32 towards Noyon. After 4.5km, turn right on the D81 across the river. Then for 31km take the D130, passing through Ollencourt. Where the road meets the D934, turn right to Blérancourt. The hotel is off a road to the left. **Airport:** *Paris (110km)* **Station:** *Noyon (14km)*

Hostellerie Le Griffon is beside the gateway to the magnificent Château de Blérancourt, which is now a museum of Franco-American friendship. The hotel itself has a small garden and a fenced-in duck pond, but there are splendid views of the château from the dining room (which in summer incorporates a covered terrace). Perhaps because the listed prices seem inexpensive, the hotel appears to be very popular with touring motorists. We found it unexceptional. Some of the bedrooms are reasonably sized. Ours, on the top floor, was very small and claustrophobic - the plumbing didn't work properly and, being immediately under the roof, it was insufferably hot. During our visit, the food was mediocre, especially an oversweet lemon meringue pie without a hint of lemon.

10 HOSTELLERIE DU CHATEAU H

♛♛ ★ ★ ★ ♥
02130 Fère-en-Tardenois,
  Aisne.
Tel: 23 82 21 13; 23 82 22 13
Telex: 145 526 F
Direc: M. Alain Fremiot
Open: All year

Twin with shower   1 D
Twin with bath   4 D
Double with bath   11 D-E
Suites (max. 4)   7 E-J
Total rooms: 23

No lift. 6 ground-floor
  rooms.

Restaurant: Open every day
Chef: M. Christophe Blot
Lunch: 12.30 - 14.00
Dinner: 19.30 - 21.00
Prix fixe: Menus at B & C
  A la carte available
Specialities: *Escalope de foie
gras aux radis noirs et
gingembre;
  Feuillantine de sandre aux
  chanterelles grises; Filet de
  boeuf à la ficelle, sauce bouzy;
  Aiguillette de perdreau et son
  feuilleté à la canelle; Chaud
  froid d'ananas.*

Seminars: max. 50
Groups: max. 40
Receptions: max. 70
Credit cards:
  American Express
  Diners Club
  Visa
English, German & Spanish
  spoken.

Helipad
Tennis court
Practice golf course
Jogging course

Relais & Châteaux

27km north-east of Château-Thierry (and its exit on Autoroute 4). Take the D967 through Fère-en-Tardenois. The château is a further 5km on the right. **Airport:** *Charles de Gaulle (102km)* **Station:** *Fère-en-Tardenois (5km) or Château-Thierry (27km)*

The eight ruined towers of the sixteenth-century castle still stand and are reached by a spectacular, although partially demolished, monumental bridge on five vast arches spanning the moat. At one time, this château belonged to Henry Montmorency, who made the mistake of plotting to overthrow Richelieu - a serious error of judgement that in 1632 lost him the château and his head. Handed back to the family by Louis XIII, the château was finally inherited by Louis Philippe, Duc d'Orleans, an excitable character who overindulged in gambling, drinking and other pleasures before throwing in his lot with the revolutionaries and changing his name to Philippe Egalité. Always one for the grand gesture, he knocked down much of his château to prove whose side he was on. It didn't help him much - his possessions were sold at public auction and he was guillotined.

The present château was rebuilt in 1863, using bits and pieces from earlier buildings. It's a vast sprawling place of three storeys, set amidst grand shrubberies and flower beds. In 1956, it was converted into a luxury hotel by the Blot family. Early in 1989, it was purchased lock-stock-and-barrel by a rich French businessman who is determined to ensure that the already high standards are further improved. Alain Fremiot, the director, leads the efficient and knowledgeable staff of fifty-five (twenty of whom work in the kitchen and dining room). Some of these have worked at the hotel for over twenty-five years and the chef, Christophe Blot, is the son of the previous owner.

Twelve of the bedrooms are in the old, central part of the hotel. They are pretty and comfortable, furnished with antiques. The other, more luxurious and expensive bedrooms, are in the side wing. All of these have considerable space and subdued, harmonised decorations. The colour scheme of ours was honey and beige and the

bathroom was bliss. Before going down to dinner, we luxuriated both in the multiple-headed shower and in the huge bath with its in-built jacuzzi.

The two parts of the dining room are elegantly furnished with everything, including the cutlery and crockery, perfectly presented. The service is both faultless and helpful. We, for example, were given much useful information about local wines. But above all, it is the food at the château that most impresses. It is invariably beautifully presented, and uses an imaginative combination of choice ingredients and fine sauces. What surprises is that at present it merits only one Michelin rosette. The menus change from lunch to dinner at the weekends and daily during the week. Apart from selecting from the card, there is a menu traditionnel and a menu degustation. The latter was our choice at the château. Not only were there three separate (but moderately-sized!) fish dishes (langoustine, mullet and turbot for our first evening), followed by a palate-cleansing sorbet, the main dish of aiguillette of duck with sweet-and-sour sauce and the cheese-board, but also two desserts. It is definitely not the place to go while on a strict diet!

Staying at the Hostellerie du Château is a magnificent experience. Of course, it is not cheap, but the setting, the atmosphere, the high standard of service, the comfort of the bedrooms, the luxury of the bathrooms, and the superb cuisine place it for us among the best hotels in France.

11 CHATEAU DE BELLINGLESE H

🛡 ★ ★

60157 Elincourt-Sainte
  Marguerite, Oise.
Tel: 44 76 04 76
Telex: 155 048 F
Fax: 44 76 54 75
Propr: Société Anonyme
Direc: M. Colin
Open: All year

Twin with shower   4 B-C
Twin with bath   27 B-E
Double with bath   13 B-E
Suites   3 F-G
  Total rooms: 47
Lift

Restaurant: Open every day
Chef: M. Michel Frey
Lunch: 1200 - 1430
Dinner: 1930 - 2130
Prix fixe: Menus at A & B
  A la carte available
Specialities: *Marbré de foie
  gras et ris de veau aux
  noisettes accompagné de sa
  marguerite de melon; Salade
  de turbotin à la menthe
  fraîche et haricots verts
  croquant au vinaigre de
  framboise.*
Demi-pension (min. 2 days)
  C

Seminars: max. 90
Groups: max. 90
Receptions: max. 100
Credit cards:
  American Express
  Diners Club
  Eurocard
  Visa
English, German & Spanish
  spoken

Tennis court
Swimming pool

Close to Autoroute 1. 16km north of Compiègne. From there, cross the River Oise on the N31. Swing left and take the first right. Swing right again and keep straight on to the N32 towards Noyon. After 1.5km, turn left onto the D142 to Elincourt-Sainte-Marguerite. The château is down a long road on the right just after the village. **Airport:** *Charles de Gaulle (45km)* **Station:** *Compiègne (16km)*

This vast, astonishing place - reflected in its own lake and set in a wooded 650-acre estate - dates back to the sixteenth century. Faced in red brick, it has a central building with two wings at right angles with two adjoining turrets. The staircase is inside another corbelled turret. There are also numerous outbuildings, including a tower which was once the fortified keep. Long before the present château was built, there was a fortified castle on the site, where, according to local legend, Joan of Arc was once imprisoned.

Used as a military hospital during the Second World War, the château was subsequently neglected. A massive and expensive programme of restoration began early in 1986 and in April 1987 Château de Bellinglise was opened as a first-class hotel. Inside, there is a warren of rooms, most of them very large. Much of the recent work has concentrated on further equipping these areas for the apparently insatiable seminar market. In eight conference-rooms, there are videos, sound-systems, projectors and other electronic gadgetry, including a satellite television receiver. Most of the restoration work has been well done - some walls have been marbled and the new furniture is in a traditional style. The bedrooms vary in size, but all have been decorated with care and flare, with plain light carpets and attractive fabric used for curtains, bed-covers and on the wall. Less pleasing is the bar with its overstated purple and puce carpet.

The wood-panelled dining room is most agreeably furnished with blue-upholstered wooden-framed seats, and circular tables covered in crisp white cloths. The cuisine of Michel Frey is first class. The reception staff were among the most efficient we encountered. Further improvements are still be undertaken, including an 18-hole golf-course. Although little remains of the atmosphere of an ancient building, Château de Bellinglise has already established a justifiably good reputation for its comfort, cuisine and efficient staff. (In 1989, reports in *The Sunday Times* claimed that the Moonies were the actual owners of this château.)

12 CHATEAU DE LA TOUR H

♟ ★
60270 Gouvieux, Oise
Tel: 44 57 07 39, 44 58 19 37
Propr: Mme Jeanne Jadas
Open: All year, except 28
   July - 12 Aug

Restaurant: Open every day
   (except 17 July - 12 Aug)
Lunch: 12.00 - 14.00
Dinner: 19.00 - 21.00
Prix fixe: Menus at A & B
   A la carte available

Seminars: max. 30
Groups: max. 25
Credit cards:
   American Express
   Visa
English and Spanish spoken

Twin with bath	6 B-C	No lift
Double with bath	8 B-C	
Suite (max. of 4)	1 C	
Total rooms:	15	

Tennis court

50km north of Paris. From there, take the N16 towards Chantilly. In Lamorlaye, turn left onto the N162 to Gouvieux, where turn right onto the D909. After 1km, turn left and the château is on the left. **Airport:** *Charles de Gaulle (42km)* **Station:** *Chantilly (3km)*

Built at the beginning of this century in a Tyrolean style, the château stands in a delightful park of 10 acres with flowers beds and a fantastic lawn. It is surrounded by a forest. The interior is attractively decorated in mainly plain but interesting colours. There is an acceptable mixture of antique and reproduction furniture. In the public rooms there are polished parquet floors. The wooden staircase leading from the hall has a carved ballustrade. The lounge and dining rooms have high, decorative ceilings and large casement windows that open out onto the terrace, where guests can drink and sunbathe. The bedrooms vary in size, but all are pleasantly decorated and furnished. (Two do not have a private w.c.)
   When we visited, the hotel had an old-fashioned, fuddy-duddy atmosphere. The welcome we received was exceptionally cool and there seemed to be a conspicuous shortage of staff. The place was not to our taste. It is, however, a reasonably well-maintained and comparatively inexpensive hotel relatively close to Paris.

13 CHATEAU DE MONTVILLARGENNE H

✠ ★ ★

Rue François Mathet, 60270
Gouvieux, Oise.
Tel: 44 57 05 14
Telex: 150 212 F
Fax: 44 58 16 37
Proprs: Groupe Méiathel
S.A.
Direc: Mlle Catherine
Peyreaud
Open: All year

Single with shower	22
Double with shower	40 B
Double with bath	115 B
Suites	3 D
Total rooms:	180

Restaurant: Open daily
Chef: M. Varoqui
Lunch: 1200 - 1330
Dinner: 1900 - 2200
Prix fixe: Menus at A & B
  A la carte available
Specialities: *Saumon frais
  saumuré aux senteurs d'aneth;
  Grenadin de veau crème de
  citron vert; Nougat glacé à la
  gelée de sauternes et coulis de
  kiwi.*

Lift. 15 ground-floor rooms.

Seminars: max. 350
Groups: max. 50
Receptions: max. 450
Credit cards:
  American Express
  Diners Club
  Eurocard
  Visa
English, German & Spanish
  spoken

Indoor swimming pool
Tennis courts
Golf course 5km

La Castellerie

11km from Senlis (and exit 8 on the A1). From there, take the D924 to Chantilly. In the town, turn left and take the D909 to Gouvieux. Just before entering the town, turn left down a well sign-posted road that leads to the château on the right. **Airport:** *Charles de Gaulle (42km)* **Station:** *Chantilly (4km)*

This is an astonishing place. Built for the Rothschild family at the end of the nineteenth century and set in a park of fourteen acres, it is a vast, rambling building that was designed to impress in a strange mixture of architectural styles. There are upper parts with brick and timber facing that are mock-medieval; but most of the grey-slated château is built of white stone with red brick decorations. After the Second World War, it housed first a girls' school and then a college for hoteliers. Since 1980, it has been an extremely busy and successful hotel.

Like all the public rooms, the carpeted entrance hall has a vast high ceiling. There are attractive white stone walls and a large sweeping flight of stairs. Overlooking the terrace and grounds, the dining rooms are wood-panelled with gilt mirrors and decorated panels. On the tables are crisp white and pink cloths and napery. In the corners are vast arrangements of fresh flowers. The food too lives up to the impression of grandeur. In 1987, the cuisine was awarded 'Le Laurier d'Or'.

And there is much, much more. There are televisions in the adequate if not overlarge bedrooms, a sauna, a boutique, billiards, a disco and organised tours of the area. Despite the large number of people milling around, a calm atmosphere prevails, especially among the receptionists. The cost of staying at the châteaux is also very reasonable. So what is the catch? There isn't one. Such a large hotel, much used by jet-setting businessmen and groups of young people, is not to everybody's taste. We have only small complaints about our visit - there was nobody to serve us in the bar at 1500 and we waited over two hours to meet a member of the management who never arrived.

14 CHATEAU D'HUMIERES H

★ ★

60113 Monchy-Humières, Oise.	Restaurant: Closed Sun evenings	Seminars: max. 12
Tel: 44 42 39 51	Lunch: 1200 - 1400	Groups: max. 12
Open: All year	Dinner: 1900 - 2230	Receptions: max. 45
Double with bath 4 B-D	Prix fixe: Menus at A & B	Credit cards:
Suites 3 D-F	A la carte available	Visa
Total rooms: 7		English spoken
(Further rooms planned)	No lift	18-hole golf course
		Tennis courts

7km south-east of exit 11 on the A1. From there, turn left onto the D935 towards Compiègne. At Monchy-Humières, turn right into the village and then take a left-turn down to the château. **Airport:** *Charles de Gaulle (45km)* **Station:** *Compiègne (8km)*

This hotel with its new 18-hole golf course opened in 1989. The château itself dates from early in the seventeenth century. In 1649, it was visited by Charles II of England, accompanied by his son, the Duke of York, during his exile in France after his father, Charles I, had been beheaded in London. The exterior of the building, with its colonnaded central section and perfect symmetry is most appealing. Inside, a considerable amount of redecoration has taken place. There is much white paintwork and light basket-work chairs and settees covered with cushions. In the sitting-room, there are artificial trees. The restaurant is simple, with stone-flag floors, white tables and chairs, bright yellow napkins and candles. The cuisine is similarly light and unpretentious. The bedrooms are spacious with plain decorations - white walls and curtains, brown carpets and colourful bedspreads. A couple of rooms, however, are bedecked with the odd animal skin. There are televisions in all the bedrooms and the bathrooms are spotless.

Most attention has been given to creating the golf-course within the 130-acre estate. The undulating course has a considerable number of water hazards and appears to offer a challenge to most golfers. André Groulx is the director of a Golf School at the course which provides both individual and group lessons.

It is still early days for this enterprise, but a considerable amount of money has already been spent and a thoughtful and helpful staff has been recruited.

---

15 CHATEAU DU ROMEREL PG

♛ ♛ ★ ★

15 Quai du Romerel, 80230
  Saint-Valery-sur-Somme,
  Somme.
Tel: 22 26 93 92
Proprs: M. & Mme François
  Knecht
Open: 1 Mar - 31 Dec (but
  closed Sun evenings)

Twin with shower	2 B
Twin with bath	2 B
Double with bath	1 B
Total rooms:	5
Apartments	2

No lift

No restaurant

No credit cards
English spoken

Swimming pool
Miniature golf course
Tennis courts 500m
Golf course 10km
Horse riding 10km

Les Etapes François Coeur

*20km north-west of Abbeville. From there, take the D925 towards Eu. After 5km, at
Cambron, turn right onto the D3 to Saint-Valery-sur-Somme.* **Airport:** *Amiens (68km)*
Station: *Noyelles (6km)*

This delightful, white manor-house was built in 1820, an annexe being added forty
years later. With a ten-acre wooded park and a beautiful view across the Bay of
the Somme, it occupies a tranquil and privileged site on the edge of the pretty,
small fishing and holiday village of Saint-Valery-sur-Somme. The château is
unspoiled and yet very comfortable, with many amenities, including a splendid,
tree-shaded swimming pool. The bedrooms are simple, but spacious and stylish,
and all overlook the bay. In the converted annexe, there are two apartments with
kitchenettes. M. and Mme Knecht are agreeable, helpful hosts who do all they can
to ensure that their guests are comfortable and content - including providing
excellent breakfasts! Occasional musical evenings are held in the grounds. By day
or in the evening - when the château is illuminated - it looks most appealing. It's
an ideal and recommended place to stay, in a little known but captivating seaside
village.

16 CHATEAU DE VAUCHELLES-LES-DOMART PG

♜ ♜ ♜

80620 Vauchelles-lés-Domart, Somme.	(Reservation desirable)		No credit cards
	Double rooms	4 B	English spoken
Tel: 22 51 62 51	Single room	1 B	
Propr: Baronne de Lassus	Total rooms	5	Tennis court
Open: 1 June - 30 Sep	No lift		
	No restaurant		Gîtes de France

28km north-west of Amiens. From there, take the N1. After 27km, at Mouflers, turn right on the D216 to Vauchelles. Turn left to the church and château. **Airport:** *Amiens (33km)* **Station:** *Abbeville (19km)*

This superb red-brick and stone château has belonged to the same family since it was built in the seventeenth century. Entry is through an imposing archway with a gatehouse on either side. A cobbled driveway sweeps round along the perpendicular wing that houses the stables and the home of the caretaker and his family. Ahead is the tall, main building of the château, with its two matching side pavilions. At the back is a formal garden with a central fountain. The fine proportions of the house and grounds perfectly complement each other. The interior is charming. Precious antiques, paintings and historical mementoes are everywhere. On the polished, old oak-floorboards are priceless rugs. There is about everything a feeling of dignity and gentility. Yet, perhaps partially because the owner lives much of the year elsewhere, the château has a quietly passive air rather than being a vibrant family house. The guest rooms vary in size, but all have large comfortable beds and rug-covered polished floorboards. Above the bed in the largest room is an impressive crucifix in blue and gilt that would cause a nasty headache if it fell on a slumbering guest! Breakfast is served in the bedrooms. A drawing room and billiard room are open to guests.

Despite being a historic monument of great importance, this château is neither well known nor frequently visited. It stands, as it has done for over three hundred years, in its beautiful, tranquil setting next to the village church, where few sounds are heard but for the song of the birds and the occasional bark of a dog.

17 CHATEAU DE WARGNIES PG

♥ ♥

Wargnies, 80670 Canaples,
  Somme.
Tel: 22 93 71 75
Propr: M. Claude de
  Francqueville
Open: All year

Double room

No lift

No restaurant

1 A

No credit cards
English spoken

Tennis court 2km
Horse riding 12km

Gîtes de France

18km north of Amiens. From there, take the D933 towards Canaples. After 17km, at Havernas, turn right onto the D60 to Wargnies, where turn right to the church and château. **Airport:** *Amiens (22km)* **Station:** *Amiens (18km) or Canaples (4km)*

The grandfather of the present owner of Château de Wargnies was the Picard painter and illustrator, Jean de Francqueville, who lived in the village for fifty years and was its mayor for forty-four. There is still one of his paintings on the cupboard door of what was his child's bedroom.

The estate is a working farm - when we visited there was a strong smell of pigs at the front of the house. The château itself is rather bare, but Mme de Francqueville is extremely friendly and helpful. Breakfast is taken en famille in the large country kitchen. There is a wonderful view over open countryside from the guest bedroom, which is clean and comfortable. The toilet facilities are fine, although the bath is small and oddly-shaped. As an extra bed can be added to the bedroom and a separate single room is available, the château is ideal for people wishing to have a cheap but agreeable family holiday amidst beautiful French countryside.

18 CHATEAU DU CLOTAY H

Ü ★ ★

8 Rue du Port, 91350 Grigny, Essonne.
Tel: 69 25 89 98
Propr: M. Williams Griguer
Open: All year

Twin with bath	15 D-E
Double with bath	5 D-E
Total rooms:	20

Restaurant: Open daily
Chef: M. Serge Chatelain
Lunch: 1200 - 1500
Dinner: 1930 - 2200
Prix fixe: Menus at B
  A la carte available
Demi-pension (3 nights+) D

No lift. 5 ground-floor rooms.

Groups: max. 40
Credit cards:
  American Express
  Diners Club
  Visa
English & Italian spoken

Swimming pool
Tennis court
Golf course 3km

7km south of Orly airport. From there (or from Paris), take the N7 and at Grigny, after passing a lake on the right, turn right into Rue du Port. The château is almost at the end on the right. **Airport:** *Orly (7km)* **Station:** *Grigny (500m)*

Purchased by M. Griguer in 1988, Château du Clotay has been entirely renovated and many improvements made. Everywhere has been attractively redecorated and fitted with new pale-coloured woollen carpet. The number of bedrooms has been doubled and all twenty of them have been given excellent new bathrooms. The garden has been replanted and new paving-stones laid. In the grounds, a most attractive fully-glassed winter garden has been constructed. Although the dining rooms are extremely pleasant, we chose to eat on the terrace overlooking the large expanse of lake. And the cuisine is excellent. We had two mouthwatering desserts - *Le chocolatier à la mousse d'oranges* and *La forêt noire glacée aux griottes*. Highly recommended!

With all the improvements that have been made and with such a splendid setting only 20km from Paris, the château is extremely popular, especially at weekends. We were there on a Sunday when three separate confirmation parties were being held and the place was full. Despite this, all the staff, including the proprietor and his charming wife, were most helpful and efficient. The exterior of the three-storeyed, grey-stone building, which was built in 1824, is rather plain. But we found nothing else to mar what is one of the best château-hotels close to Paris.

19 HOSTELLERIE DE VILLEMARTIN

H

⚜ ★

4 Allee des Marronniers,
Morigny, 91150 Etampes,
Essonne.
Tel: 64 94 63 54
Propr: M. Michel Savignet
Open: All year, except Aug
Closed Sun eves & Mon

Twin with shower	5 B
Twin with bath	3 B
Double with shower	3 B
Double with bath	3 B
Total rooms:	14

No lift. 2 ground-floor
rooms.

Restaurant: Closed
Sun eves & Mon
Chef: M. Xavier Rabault
Lunch: 1200 - 1330
Dinner: 2000 - 2130
Prix fixe: Menus at A & B
A la carte available
Specialities: *Filet de sole au
safran; Terrine de lotte aux
feuilles d'estragon; Les trois
mignons en arc en ciel;
L'effeuillé de pommes coulis
framboises.*

Seminars: max. 30
Groups: max. 25
Receptions: max. 30
Credit cards:
American Express
Diners Club
Eurocard
Visa
English & Spanish spoken

Tennis court
Golf course 4km

48km south of Paris. Take the N20. Leave at Etrechy, following the D148 under the N20. Then turn right onto the D17. The château is on the right. **Airport:** *Orly (30km)* **Station:** *Etampes (1.5km)*

This attractive white-stone château was a fortified farmhouse, built during the sixteenth century. The facade has slatted-shutters at each of its many windows. A double flight of steps leads to the front door. Set in a wooded, forty-acre park, beside the River Juine, it is charming and peaceful. The interior decorations are less so. Brown and orange nylon carpet appears to be everywhere, as does a deep pink patterned wallpaper. The bedrooms are divided into two categories - 'grand confort' and 'bon confort'. The former are large with commodious bathrooms; the latter are much smaller and have tiny bathrooms with a shower. All the bedrooms have either wallpaper or fabric in bold swirling patterns, though in relatively subdued colours. However, all the staff are most pleasant and helpful. The restaurant is attractive and the cuisine, specialising in regional dishes, is good. Everywhere is comfortable and immaculate. The château is an inexpensive and extremely popular retreat, close to Paris.

20 CHATEAU DE CHAUMONTEL

H

☺ ★ ★

21 Rue Andre Vassord,
  Chaumontel, 95270
  Luzarches, Val-d'Oise.
Tel: 34 71 00 30
Telex: 609 730 F
Proprs: M. and Mme Rigard
Open: All year

Twin with shower	4 B
Twin with bath	12 B
Double with bath	2 B
Suites	2 D
Total rooms:	20

Restaurant: Open every day
Lunch: 1200 - 1415
Dinner: 1900 - 2130
Prix fixe: Menu at A
  A la carte available
Specialities: *Raclette de filet de
  canard; Assiette de poissons
  marinés; Flan de pintadeau au
  cacao amer.*
Demi-pension (3 days+) D-E

No lift. 1 ground-floor room.

Seminars: max. 25
Groups: max. 20
Credit cards:
  American Express
  Visa

Tennis court 500m
Horse riding 1km
Swimming pool 9km

32km north-east of Paris. Take the N 16 to Luzarches and, when almost through the town, turn right to Chaumontel. The château is a further 500m. **Airport:** *Charles de Gaulle (22km)* **Station:** *Luzarches (2km)*

Built as a hunting-lodge for the Prince of Condé in the sixteenth century, this moated château was susbsequently much enlarged and altered. Despite the resulting jumble of styles - ancient round towers and an impressive, classical entrance - it is a most attractive building, set in a park of ancient trees. It has been used as a location for numerous films.

M. and Mme Rigard became the new proprietors in 1987 and have introduced many changes. The garden is immaculate with barely a leaf out of place and the flower-beds are planted in regimental rows. The exterior walls have been cleaned and painted so that the château looks as though it has been newly built. Inside, the atmosphere is similarly prim. The reception we received was decidedly chilly. Perhaps we called on an off-day. Certainly, the place was exceptionally busy.

There is a delightful terrace where drinks and meals are served. Inside, there are fresh flowers everywhere. All the bedrooms are different. Beneath the eaves, there are rooms, arched with heavy beams; on the floor below, there are elegant bedrooms in the eighteenth-century style. All are comfortable and well furnished.

21 CHATEAU DE MAFFLIERS H

♥ ★ ★

Maffliers, 95560 Montsoult, Val-d'Oise.
Tel: 34 73 93 05
Telex: 695 701 F
Propr: A Novotel Hotel
Direc: M. Jean-Jacques Guillemin
Open: All year

Twin rooms with shower
  80 C
  (All rooms in an annexe)
Lift in the annexe
  28 ground floor rooms.

Restaurant: Open daily
Lunch: 12.00 - 14.30
Dinner: 19.00 - 22.00
Prix fixe: Menus at A & B
  A la carte available
Specialities: *Foie gras de canard frais et son verre de Sauternes; Mille-feuille de saumon frais au beurre safrané.*

Seminars: max. 180
Groups: max. 160
Receptions: max. 200
Credit cards:
  American Express
  Diners Club
  Eurocard
  Visa
English, German, Italian & Spanish spoken

Swimming pool
Tennis courts
Horse riding
Golf course 10km

29km north of Paris. Take the N1 and at Maffliers turn right. Take the first left and then the first right, which leads to the château. **Airport:** *Charles de Gaulle (25km)* **Station:** *Montsoult (500m)*

There have been several châteaux at Maffliers. The fifteenth-century one was destroyed in the Wars of Religion; the next was razed during the French Revolution. In the nineteenth century, the present château was built in the classical style by the Talleyrand-Perigord family. When it was acquired by the Novotel group, it was decided that the grandeur of neither the building nor the grounds would be spoiled. The comfortable accommodation was put in a nearby annexe and the rooms in the château were carefully restored. Almost all of these are now seminar rooms which, at least for independent travellers, is a waste. If you do visit the hotel, make sure that you see at least the Salon Fresques, with its fantastic painted ceiling and ornately carved woodwork. Numerous facilites are provided for guests, including the swimming pool, tennis court and gymnasium. The hotel annexe lacks atmosphere, but the terrace restaurant in the château is attractive with the feel of a busy, modern Parisian café. The food, though expensive, is very good.

22 CHATEAU DE LA CORNICHE H

★ ★

Route de la Corniche,
  Rolleboise, 78270
  Bonnières-sur-Seine,
  Yvelines.
Tel: 30 93 21 24
Telex: 695 544 F
Fax: 30 42 27 77
Proprs: M. Jean-Louis
  Bourrier & Mme Olga
  Ternova-Bourrier
Open: All year, but closed
  Sun evenings & Mon from
  1 Oct - 30 April

Lift. 1 ground-floor room.

Twin with shower	7 C
Twin with bath	16 C-D
Double with shower	2 C-D
Double with bath	13 B-D
Suite (max. 4)	1 G-D
Total rooms:	39

(22 of the rooms are in the
château)

Restaurant: Closed Sun
  evenings & Mon from
  1 Oct - 30 April
Chef: M. Eric Ciquel
Lunch: 1230 - 1430
Dinner: 1930 - 2130
Prix fixe: Menus at A & B
  A la carte available

Seminars: max. 50
Groups: max. 20
Receptions: max. 180
Credit cards:
  American Express
  Diners Club
  Visa
English & Spanish spoken

Swimming pool
Tennis court
Horse riding 5km
Golf course 20km

Châteaux Hôtels Indép.
Relais du Silence

9km north-west of Mantes-la-Jolie (and exit from Autoroute 13). Take the N13 towards Bonnières-sur-Seine. The château is on the right after 9km. **Airport:** *Paris (75km)* **Station:** *Mantes-la-Jolie (9km)*

Gone are the days when kings could openly build mansions for their mistresses which, when they've served their purpose (the building, that is) could be turned into posh hotels where the conservative bourgeoisie could for the odd night live vicariously. Château de la Corniche was built towards the end of the nineteenth century by the pioneer jet-setter, King Leopold II of Belgium, as a less than discreet hide-away for his mistress, Baronne de Vaughan. After she'd borne him two children, he did the decent thing and married her in 1909 - three days before he died.

The château was turned into a hostellerie in 1922 and was instantly successful. Perched high above a bend of the Seine and just off the main road to Paris it was in an ideal position. But since then, there's been a World War, the exploits of Leopold II have been forgotten, the autoroute has been built and tastes have changed. The château has passed through different hands who've met with success and setbacks. The hotel changed ownership again in 1987 and had a new chef.

The interior of the hotel is disappointing - it has a stuffy old-fashioned look, with lots of oak panelling, heavy carved oak bannisters and a swirling gold and brown carpet. The bedrooms are pleasant but a little ordinary. Ours was small and very hot, with deep red walls and white cotton bedspread. The restaurant is the most interesting area in the château. At its entrance, there is a statue fountain. The room itself is furnished with modern moulded chairs and tables covered with pretty pink cloths. There is a bonsai tree on each table. From the terrace and some of the rooms there are amazing views across the Seine. We found the place rather formal and not particularly welcoming. We welcome reports.

23 PAVILLON HENRI IV H

🛡🛡 ★ ★
21 Rue Thiers, 78100 Saint-
  Germaine-en-Laye,
Yvelines.
Tel: 34 51 62 62
Telex: 695 822 F
Fax: 39 73 93 73
Propr: M. René Brulé
Direc: M. Soret
Open: All year

Single with bath	12 F
Double with bath	30 G
Suites	3 G-J
Total rooms:	45

Lift

Restaurant: Open daily
Lunch: 1215 - 1430
Dinner: 1900 - 2230
A la carte

Seminars: max. 270
Groups: max. 50
Receptions: max. 180
Credit cards:
  American Express
  Diners Club
  Visa
English & German spoken

Inter. Leading Association

31km east of the centre of Paris. From there, cross the Seine at Neuilly-sur-Seine and then take the N186 to Saint-Germain-en-Laye. Just before entering the town, the road again crosses the Seine and (then called Avenue de Lattre) bends sharply to the right and then to the left. At the first roundabout, turn right into Avenue Gambetta. At the end, turn right into Rue Thiers. The château is at the bottom on the left. **Airport:** *Orly (40km)* **Station:** *Saint-Germain-en-Laye*

Pavillon Henri IV, which was once the king's chapel, is the only substantial remnant of the vast Château Neuf, the royal palace completed in 1604 during the reign of Henri IV. The rest was finally destroyed during the Revolution. After years of neglect, the chapel was taken over in the middle of the nineteenth century by the renowned restaurateur Collinet, the creator of béarnaise sauce, who renamed the building Hotel du Pavillon Henri IV. Alexandre Dumas was one of his many famous customers. With its spectacular, panoromaic view of Paris, it is still an expensive hotel with some style. The attractive and spacious entrance hall has oriental carpets on the floor and beautiful plaques on the wall. Placed around are ornate, French antiques. There is a delightful breakfast room with a painted dome and marquetry floor. The food is good and the service courteous. But at the time of our visit the grandeur was a little faded - fresh flowers were wilting, the wooden floor needed polishing and some of the walls badly needed a fresh coat of paint.

24 CHATEAU DE THOIRY PG

♥♥♥ ★ ★ ♥
78770 Thoiry-en-Yvelines
Tel: 34 87 52 25
Telex: 699 050 F
Fax: 34 87 54 12
Propr: Vicomte de la
   Panouse
Direc: Annabelle Vicomtesse
   de la Panouse
Open: All year (but
   reservation essential)

Single with bath	1 E	
Double with bath	3 H-R	
Suites (max. 3)	2 R-W	
(including breakfast)		
Total rooms:	6	

No lift

Table d'hôte on request H

Credit cards:
   American Express
   Diners Club
   Visa
English & Spanish spoken

Wild life reserve
Museum of Gastronomy

Inter. Leading Association

40km east of Paris. Leave by Porte Auteuil and take the A13, leaving it after 12km to take the A12 to Versailles. There turn right onto the N12 to Pontchartrain. Shortly afterwards, turn right on the D11 to Thoiry. The château is in the village on the left. **Airport:** *Orly (46km)* **Station:** *Pontchartrain (10.5km)*

Everything about Château de Thoiry, including the price of a night's stay, is amazing, perhaps even outrageous. Yet the building is so spectacular, the contents so magnificent, the grounds so beautiful and the place so full of life and activity that it is unforgettable. Even if, like us, you couldn't afford to stay or dine there, it is certainly well worth a visit. For over four hundred years, the château has been a family residence and the present Comte de La Panouse is a descendent of the original owner who had the building constructed in 1564. The architect, Philibert de L'Orme, designed Thoiry according to the rules of the golden number and the traditions of the Knights Templar. The building's position was carefully selected and the two windows on either side of the central door on the south-west side were placed at increasingly wider intervals than the windows opposite. As a result, the five windows on the ground floor of the building produce a luminous bridge of light. This is most marked during the winter and summer solstices, when from the terrace the sun can be seen to set or rise framed by the great door of the grand vestibule.

Hostellerie du Château (10) Aisne (Picardy)

Château des Crayères (27) Marne (Champagne)

The house itself is full of priceless treasures. In the Green Drawing Room is a piano on which Chopin played. The manuscript of the two waltzes he dedicated to Clemence de Marquet, Comtesse de La Panouse, is on display in the château's Archives Museum, which also includes hundreds of letters from royalty, statesmen and writers. On the walls of the main staircase there is a series of five rare nineteenth-century Gobelin tapestries representing 'The Loves of the Gods'. In the White Library Drawing Room with its fine collection of books dating from the sixteenth century there is an eighteenth-century pink rock crystal chandelier. On all the walls there are family portraits by artists such as Largillère, de La Tour and Ozane. There are Louis XV armchairs and a harpsichord dating from 1733, gilded French Regency furniture and magnificent tapestries - all having been in the family for generations. Also in the house is a Museum of Gastronomy, including re-creations of spectacular desserts, manuscripts and a collection of antique utensils.

From the château can be seen the extraordinary French gardens designed by Le Nôtre and his nephew, Desgot. There are also three hundred acres of English parkland gardens. Then there is the vast zoological park - the first to be opened in Europe - with its African reserve in which there are over a thousand specimens of twenty-one species, a bear park with over sixty bears and a lion park. Alongside are all the attendant amenities - tea rooms, children's playgrounds and a restaurant.

A vast variety of additional activities can also be arranged at Thoiry. If you've got the money and it's to your taste, you can drink champagne in the Lion House, attend a pastry-decoration demonstration, attend an African Night party, or buy a pot of the Vicomtesse's unusual home-made jams, including one made from carrot, pine-nut and whiskey.

These 'amusing extras', as she describes them, are the ideas of Annabelle, Vicomtesse de La Panouse. An American from Minnesota, she was formerly a cover-girl until she married the present Vicomte. With her infectious torrent of laughter she brings fun and considerable verve to her work as the château's commercial director. She has supervised all the considerable work that has taken place on redecorating and refurbishing the bedrooms that can be rented in the château. All are most lavish, with wide swags, bows and trims of specially printed cloth. The mirrors have been regilded, the walls covered in exquisite padded material. In the bathroom there are antique marble washstands. And for those not content merely to be spending a night in such a lavishly equipped bedroom in one of France's most historic ancestral homes, they can also, at a considerable price, enjoy a banquet with the Vicomte and Vicomtesse. It will be an incredibly expensive but most unusual experience.

25 CHATEAU DE VILLEPREUX PG

♥♥♥ ★

78450 Villepreux, Yvelines.

Tel: 30 56 20 05

Telex: 689 185 F

Fax: 30 56 12 12

Propr: Comtesse de Saint
   Seine

Open: All year (on
   reservation

Single with shower	2 C	
Single with bath	4 C	
Twin with bath	5 E	
Double with bath	1 E	
Total rooms:	12	
No lift		
Table d'hôte on res. A		

Groups: max. 12

No credit cards

English spoken

Tennis court

Swimming pool 5km

Horse riding 5km

Château Accueil

20km west of Paris. From there, leave by Porte de Châtillon, taking the N306. After 13km, this feeds into the A86. Turn right for Versailles. At the end of the motorway (when the dual-carriageway becomes the N286) leave by the exit for Versailles. Turn left onto the N10. After 4km, at the end of the dual carriageway, take the D11. 2km after going underneath the autoroute, turn right onto the D11E to Villepreux. Turn left into the village and then first right. The château is a little further on the right. **Airport:** *Orly (25km)* **Station:** *Villepreux*

Almost in the back garden of the Palace of Versailles, this beautiful, elegant château was rebuilt on an old site by the Francini brothers, who designed the fountains at Versailles. Their sons built the equally spectacular fountains at Fontainebleau. They died without a male heir and, in 1768, their château was bought as a hunting lodge by Louis XV and absorbed into the royal estate. In more troubled times, Louis XVI sold Villepreux to his Curator of Buildings, a certain M. Heurtier, who may have been somewhat miffed at the high price he had to pay, because he became one of the three main conspirators against the King in the run-up to the French Revolution. Some years afterwards, the château was bought by M. Martine, who married the female descendent of the Francinis who owned the surrounding farm. So the whole estate was restored to the family of the original builders. On several subsequent occasions, daughters inherited Villepreux and through them the present owner, Comtesse de Saint Seine, is descended from the Francinis. Over the centuries many famous people have stayed at the château, and rooms there are named after them. So it is possible to sleep in the bedroom of Châteaubriand or even of Madame de Pompadour. They are all comfortable, furnished with antiques, but unmodernised. There are tiny, basic bathrooms and shared toilets - the two at one end of the long, upper corridor have on the shelves a splendid collection of books.

Comtesse de Saint Seine is a most charming lady who loves her home. She was kind enough to show her stupendous art collection, which includes a large Rubens and many fascinating family portraits. Although she doesn't speak English, her extremely helpful and pleasant daughter does. Some people may be put off by the dated sanitary arrangements. It is also vital to have the use of a car while staying at Villepreux. But these are the smallest of considerations when one has the opportunity of staying - at a price - in an authentic eighteenth-century château.

26 CHATEAU DE VILLIERS-LE-MAHIEU H

✇ ★ ★	Twin with bath	12 C	Seminars: max. 25
78770 Villiers-le-Mahieu,	Double with bath	6 C	Groups: max 25
Yvelines.	Total rooms:	18	No credit cards
Tel: 34 87 44 25			English spoken
Propr: M. Jean-Luc Chaufour	No lift		Tennis court
Open: All year, except	Table d'hôte (min of 6) on		Fishing
1 - 20 Aug	reservation B		Golf course 15km

40km west of Paris. Leave by Porte Auteuil and take the A13, leaving it after 12km to take the A12 to Versailles. There turn right onto the N12 to Pontchartrain. Shortly afterwards, turn right on the D11 and 9km later, after passing through Thoiry, turn left to the village of Villiers-le-Mahieu. The château is on the left in the village. **Airport:** *Orly (45km)* **Station:** *Garancières (8km)*

The owners claim that at Villiers-le-Mahieu guests can prepare for the twenty-first century in a château of the middle ages. The thirteenth century part is superb. The three long, ivy-covered wings flank a formal courtyard; on the fourth side is a wall decorated with life-size stone statues. The whole is totally surrounded by a wide, deep moat. At intervals on the outside of the buildings are neat round towers, sunk deep into the murky water. A tree-lined drive leads to the château and visitors enter through a tall, impressive keep. The beautifully maintained grounds are full of lawns and decorative trees. It is what has been done to prepare for the twenty-first century that somewhat disappoints. Catering mainly for seminars, conferences and receptions, the interior of the château lacks atmosphere. Yet everything has been done well. In all the conference rooms there is modern, high-quality furniture. The bedrooms are very pretty - discreetly decorated in toned colours. The smaller rooms are furnished with English pine, while in the larger ones there are interesting antique pieces. And all the bathrooms are excellent. The staff are kind and helpful. But, although the château is full of bustle, much of the life seems to have drained away, long before the twenty-first century has even started.

Chateau de Villiers-le-Mahieu (26)

27 CHATEAU DES CRAYÈRES H

Restaurant Boyer

✪ ✪ ★ ★ ★ ♀

64 Boulevard Henry Vasnier,
  51100 Reims, Marne.
Tel: 26 82 80 80
Telex: 830 959 F
Fax: 26 82 65 52
Propr: M. Gérard & Mme
  Elayane Boyer
Direc: M. Gérard Boyer
Open: 16 Jan - 20 Dec

Twin with bath   5 E-H
Double with bath   11 E-H
Suites   3 I-J
  Total rooms: 19

Lift

Restaurant: Closed all Mon &
  Tues lunch
Chef: M. Gérard Boyer
Lunch: 1200 - 1400
Dinner: 1930 - 2130
A la carte   C - D
Specialities: *Le feuilleté
  d'asperges vertes aux huitres;
  Le filet de St Pierre aux
  endives; La suprême de turbot
  à l'essence de champignons
  des bois; Le pigeon simplement
  roti, compote au chou; Le
  gratin d'ananas et le
  millefeuille aux framboises.*

Seminars: max. 25
Groups: max. 25
Credit cards:
  American Express
  Diners Club
  Eurocard
  Visa
English, German, Italian &
  Spanish spoken

Tennis court
Helipad
Swimming pool 1km
Golf course 5km

Relais & Chateaux

In Reims. From the A4, leave by the Reims exit and at the first roundabout (Place des Droits-de-l'Homme), take the first right (Avenue Gal. Giraud). The château is on the left at the junction with Boulevard Henry Vasnier. **Airport:** *Reims (5km)* **Station** *(Reims 2km)*

Château des Crayères or, as it is usually known, 'Restaurant Boyer' is one of the best hotels in Europe. Not only is the proprietor, Gérard Boyer, one of France's most renowned chefs whose cuisine fully merits its three Michelin rosettes, but the setting is both beautiful and elegant. Standing on a hill overlooking the ancient city of Reims, the white stone château is surrounded by seventeen acres of parkland with manicured lawns and neatly trimmed shrubs. The interior is sumptuously furnished, great love and care having been lavished on every detail.

Using earth brought to Reims on barges, the park of Crayères, which originally covered over a hundred and twenty acres, was constructed between 1872 and 1885 by Madame Pommery. It was intended that the terraces, designed like a spiralling shell, would provide a sight of the cathedral and the Basilique Saint-Rémy while keeping the rest of the town hidden. Between 1902 and 1904, the château was constructed in the park by Madame Pommery's daughter, the Marquise de Polignac. Her son, Melchior, Marquis de Polignac, who was a member of the International Olympic Committee and a great socialite, lived in the château between 1910 and 1940. During the Second World War, the German army built a blockhaus in the park to be used as a radio centre. Afterwards, the United Sates Army turned the château into a detention centre and cemented over the terrace so it could be used as a dance-floor. After eight years of restoration, the château became the home of Prince Guy de Polignac, who lived there until 1980. A few years later, Gérard Boyer, who'd run his successful restaurant in Reims since 1961, acquired the château and after extensive refurbishment opened it as the new Restaurant Boyer.

The elegance of the interior is apparent as soon as one enters the spacious reception area with its inlaid floor, marble pillars and carpeted staircase with an intricate wrought-iron ballustrade. Each of the guestrooms is different in appearance, but all are delightfully decorated with pastel carpets and matching fabrics. All have excellent bathrooms and overlook the park. The rooms at the back have access to a pleasant balcony. Downstairs, there is a comfortable lounge and a British bar, complete with leather-upholstered tub chairs and bar stools. But the centre-point of the château is the restaurant. It is beautifully furnished with wooden-framed arm-chairs, upholstered in a deep brown fabric that blends with the autumnal shades of the carpet. The walls have decorated wooden panels and a large tapestry. As in the rest of the château, pretty flower arrangements add splashes of colour. The beautifully laid tables, the quality of the service and the superb wine-list fittingly accompany Gérard Boyer's grande cuisine. Apart from expense, there is but one problem with eating at Restaurant Boyer - how on earth do you make a choice from the extensive card? For example, when we visited, there were thirteen hors d'oeuvres and, not counting the sorbets, eighteen desserts. As there is a limited number of places in the dining room, it is essential to make a reservation. Strongly recommended.

Chateau des Crayères (27)

28 CHATEAU DE BAREMBACH H

♛ ★ ★

5 Rue du Maréchal de Lattre,
 Barembach, 67130
 Schirmeck, Bas-Rhin.
Tel: 88 97 97 50
Telex: 800 400 F
Propr: M. Erwin & Mme
 Bente Clement
Open. All year

No lift

Single with bath	3 B
Twin with bath	8 C-D
Double with bath	4 C-D
Total rooms:	15

Restaurant: Open daily
Chef: Mlle Jocelyn Bayer
Lunch: 1200 - 1500
Dinner: 1900 - 2200
Prix fixe: Menus at A & B
A la carte available
Specialities: *Poissons griarde.*
Demi-pension   A

Seminars: max. 30
Groups: max. 20
Credit cards:
 American Express
 Diners Club
 Eurocard
 Visa
English, German & Danish
 spoken.
Tennis court
Skiing 15km
Horse riding 20km
Golf course 40km

50km south-west of Strasbourg. From there, take the A35 (E25). After 15km, continue onto the A352, which after 9.5km becomes the D392. After 25km, just before Schirmeck, take the road on the left to Barenbach. **Airport:** *Strasbourg (40km)* **Station:** *Molsheim (25km)*

Built in 1892, Château de Barembach is surrounded by mountains that in winter provide ski-runs and during the rest of the year delightful walks. In the Second World War, the château was used as a headquarters during the Rhine battles by General Patton of the United States and General la Lattre de Tasigny of France. In 1983, after much restoration, the Clement family turned their home into a small hotel which still retains many of the features and atmosphere of a turn-of-the-century country house. The rooms downstairs have rug-covered, polished parquet floors. In the reception area, there is a heavy wooden staircase, upholstered cane furniture and leaded windows. As in other public rooms, the walls are partially covered with cream-painted wood-panelling and a chandelier hangs from the ceiling with its ornamental plaster-work. The bedrooms are comfortable and the bathrooms modern. There is a sitting-room and bar for the guests. The quality of the food is good and the proprietors are extremely kind and helpful. They're happy to arrange tours of the area and will even pick you up in their car from Strasbourg airport.

29 CHATEAU D'ISENBOURG H

✇ ★ ★ ★
68250 Rouffach, Haut-Rhin.
Tel: 89 49 63 53
Telex: 880 819 F
Propr: M. René Traversac,
  Grandes Etapes Francaise
Direc: M. Dalibert
Open: 10 March - 5 Jan

Twin with bath	19 D-F
Double with bath	18 D-F
Duplex (max. 4)	1 G
Suites	2 G-H
Total rooms:	40

  (9 in a modern addition)

Lift. 3 ground-floor rooms.

Restaurant: Open daily
Lunch: 1215 - 1400
Dinner: 1915 - 2115
Prix fixe: Menus at B
  A la carte available
Chef: M. Alain Sinkbeiner
Specialities: *Millefeuille de foie
  gras chaude au céleri et
  pomme fruit; Crème d'ail aux
  truffe; Pigeon façon Isenbourg;
  Tarte chaud au chocolat au
  coulis de noix de coco.*
Demi-pension   D-E

Seminars: max. 50
Groups: max. 30
Credit cards
  Access
  American Express
  Eurocard
  Visa
English, German & Spanish
  spoken

Swimming pool
Tennis court
Horse riding 1km
Golf course 25km

Relais & Châteaux

*15 km south of Colmar. From there, take the N83 (direction Cernay) and take the Rouffach
exit.* **Airport:** *Colmar (18km)* **Station:** *Colmar (15km) or Rouffach*

Alsace seems constantly to have been in the wars. No wonder there are so few
castles left; certainly the only one worth going out of one's way to stay in is
Château d'Isenbourg. But it's not an ancient building - its forerunners were
erected, captured and demolished with monotonous regularity by almost all the
armies of Europe, including, in 1634, the Swedes.

Even earlier, on Easter Day in 1106, while Château d'Isenbourg was occupied by
Henry V of Germany, a beautiful young girl from Rouffach, while on her way to
mass, was abducted by an officer of the guard and taken to the château. Failing
to obtain her release, her mother turned in anguish to the women of the village.
They armed themselves with what weapons they could find, stormed the castle,
overpowered the guards, released the girl and seized the royal insignia - the
crown, the standard and the orb and sceptre. These were taken in triumph to the

---

church of Notre-Dame, where they were laid on the altar. From that time on, up to the present day, the women of Rouffach have always sat on the right-hand side of the church. Legend also has it that King Henry V was so angry that he set fire to the town.

Some of the present château was built around 1822. Towards the end of the last century, what was little more than a simple country house was considerably enlarged. A round tower was added at the southern end, as was an extra wing with a square tower at the northern end. Standing on a hill overlooking the picturesque town of Rouffach, the château looks especially attractive at night when the courtyard and ornamental pond are floodlit. The interior is almost Edwardian in style with comfortable but slightly frumpy rooms full of dralon-upholstered furniture, painted plaster ceilings, wood-block floors and heavily patterned carpets. The sun room has green-painted cane furniture and floral wallpaper and curtains that somewhat clash with the patterned tiled floor. The bedrooms are more stylish with pleasantly matching curtains, bed-drapes and wallpaper. The dining room is in a vaulted fifteenth-century cellar - the only substantial remnant of earlier buildings. The food is extremely good and it is to be anticipated that Alain Sinkbeiner, the chef, will win the same acclaim as his predecessors.

Isenbourg is a pleasurable place to stay. The efficient staff make guests feel welcome. For those not satisfied with just drinking and eating on the delightful terrace, there are other amusements. There is a swimming pool and tennis court in the grounds and on certain weekends between October and April there are musical evenings that end with a candlelit dinner.

30 CHATEAU D'ADOMENIL H

⚐ ★ ★

Rehainviller, 54300
  Lunéville,
  Meurthe-et-Moselle.
Tel: 83 74 04 81
Propr: M. Michel Million
Open: 1 March - 31 Jan,
  but closed Sun evenings
  & Mon

Double with bath   7 B-C
No lift

Restaurant: Closed Sun
  evenings & Mon
Lunch: 1245 - 1345
Dinner: 2000 - 2130
Prix fixe: Menus at A & B
  A la carte available
Chef: M. Michel Million
Specialities: *Salade de
  grenouilles à la menthe;
  Sandre aux lardons et gris de
  Toul; Crêpes soufflées à la
  mirabelle.*

Credit cards:
  American Express
  Visa
English & German spoken

Les Cuisiniers et Hôteliers
  de Métier

35km south-east of Nancy. From there, take the N4 to Lunéville. At the entrance to the town, turn right onto the ring-road (the D31) and then take the second on the right - it's a narrow road which crosses the river. Immediately afterwards, at the T-junction, turn left onto road which leads to the château. **Airport:** *Nancy (32km)* **Station:** *Lunéville (5km)*

It is exciting and satisfying to come across a château, run primarily as a restaurant by its famous chef/owner, that is delightfully decorated throughout and where the small number of bedrooms are luxurious and elegant. The château was built in the seventeenth century. With its four square corner-towers and the central section all having three storeys, it has a pleasing uniformity. The large picture windows on the lower two floors were introduced during the late nineteenth century. There is also a delightful hexagonal chapel, with a splendid ornamental cupola atop its sloping roof. In the pretty wooded grounds there is a small lake. It is a serene spot, apparently in the middle of open countryside and yet only a few minutes drive from a busy town.

But it is the food for which the paeons of praise must be reserved. The château opened in 1980, and since then Michel Million has built an impressive reputation - and gained a Michelin rosette. We add our praise - and not just for the food, but also for the splendid arrangements. Five delightful, well furnished and cosy salons provide the sixty available place settings. No wonder reservations are essential!

31 CHATEAU D'ALTEVILLE PG

🛡️ 🛡️ ★
Tarquimpol, 57260 Dieuze,
  Moselle.
Tel: 87 86 92 40
Proprs: M. Livier & Mme
  Marie Barthélémy.
Open: All year

Twin with bath	5 C
Double with bath	3 C
Suite (max. 4)	1 D
Total rooms:	9

No lift. 2 ground-floor
  rooms.

Table d'hôte on
  reservation

Seminars: max. 30
Groups: max. 30
Receptions: max. 80
No credit cards
English & German spoken

Horse riding 8km

Château Accueil

50km east of Nancy. From there, take the N74. After 26km, at the major fork, turn right onto the D38 through Moyenne to Dieuze, where turn right onto the D999. After 5 km, turn left on the D199f. After 1.5km do not turn right to Tarquimpol, but carry on a further 1km to the château, which is on the right. **Airport:** *Nancy (52km)* **Station:** *Sarrebourg (28km)*

Situated on the eastern French border, Château d'Alteville has several times been the home of French generals. The original part of the now substantial property was constructed as a farm-house in 1565. A hundred years later, it was acquired by the Mayor of Dieuze, an ex-cavalry officer, who added a chapel. In 1718, opposite the old house, a new, more spacious château was built. This was further enlarged after 1779, when it was the home of Nicolas Leclerc, the farmer general of Lorraine. In 1819, after the Revolution, the property passed to Victor Aimé, Baron Grandjean d'Alteville, who was aide de camp to Maréchal Moutin, Comte de Lobau. The Baron's daughter, who inherited the property, married yet another general and they further extended the property by adding the two side-wings.

In 1906, Château d'Alteville was bought by the grand-father of the present owner, M. Livier Barthélémy. He is a farmer and the Mayor of Tarquimpol. In 1958, he and his wife first opened their home to individuals and groups wishing to stay in and explore the area, which is next to the Mosellan lakes. Over the last few years, considerable improvements have been made by the Barthélémys and their children to the guest rooms. The château provides an opportunity to stay in a comfortable home with a charming, courteous and very helpful French family.

32 CHATEAU D'EPENOUX PG

♛ ♛ ★
Epenoux-Pusy, 70000 Vesoul,
  Haute-Saône.
Tel: 84 75 19 60
Propr: Mme Germaine
  Gauthier
Open: All year

No lift

Twin with bath   2 B
Double with bath   2 B
Suite (max. 3)   1 B
  (inc. breakfast)
  Total rooms: 5
Table d'hôte on
  reservation   A
Demi-pension (3 days+)   B

Credit cards:
  American Express
English & German spoken

Tennis court 1km
Swimming pool 3km

Les Etapes François Coeur

4.5km north of Vesoul. From there, take the D10 (in the direction of Saint-Loup-sur-Semouse) to Epenoux. **Station:** *Vesoul (4.5km)*

Although built close to the road, this elegant château has a large park containing many varieties of trees — limes, maples, chestnuts, firs, sycamores, and a three-hundred-year-old weeping-beech that is claimed to be unique in Europe for its height and the spread of its foliage. The château was built in the eighteenth century for the Comte d'Evereaux. The principal building has an elegant, symmetrical facade, with a central towered-entrance. Dating from the seventeenth century, there are stables, a tack-room, an orangery and a pretty chapel. The interior of the château is delightfully decorated in delicate pastels and furnished with charming antiques. Many of the rooms have sparkling crystal chandeliers. The bedrooms are light and comfortable, with rug-covered polished wooden floors and sprays of flowers on elegant side-tables. The table d'hôte is very good and special dinners are held for Christmas and New Year. There is also a fancy-dress evening on Mardi-Gras (Shrove Tuesday) and 15 August. For more mundane days, billiard and table-tennis tables are provided for guests. There are also exhibitions of paintings, sculptures and photographs by artists from the region. Mme Gauthier is a charming and considerate hostess who gives her guests a warm and friendly welcome.

33 CHATEAU DE MALANS PG

♥ ♥ ★ ★	Twin with shower	1 B	Groups: max. 10
Malans, 70140 Pesmes,	Twin with bath	2 B	No credit cards
Haute-Saône.	Double with shower	1 B	English, German & Spanish
Tel: 84 31 23 19	Double with bath	1 B	spoken
Propr: M. Guy Hoyet	(inc. breakfast)		
Open: 15 May - 30 Sep	Total rooms:	5	Swimming pool
			Fishing
No lift	Table d'hôte on		
	reservation A		Les Etapes François Coeur

24km north-east of Dole (and its exit on Autoroute 36). From there, take the D475 to Pesmes, where turn right on the D181 for 2km to Malans. The château is off to the right.
Airport: *Dole (30km)* **Station:** *Dole (12km)*

An odd hexagonal tower dominates the facade of the château. Looking a little like a light-house, it has a circular balcony and a bell-tower on top of its sharply-pointed, slated turret. The main entrance is to the left, up a double sweep of stone steps. The château was built at the end of the sixteenth century. In 1850 it was restored by Napoleon III's ambassador to China, but in 1881 it was abandoned and remained empty until it was occupied by German soldiers during the Second World War. Twenty-five years later, it was acquired by the present owner who undertook the enormous task of restoring and redecorating each of the château's twenty-five rooms.

He has accomplished a minor miracle. Each room is heavily ornamented with detailed plaster work; covering the floors is intricate parquet; there are arches and alcoves, stained glass and elaborate columns, mirrors and chandeliers. As nowhere is cluttered with furniture and the colours are soft and simple, the resulting effect is most effective. M. Hoyet has lived all over the world, and many of the rooms contain souvenirs and furniture collected in many exotic places. Although Malans is not a hotel, there are many facilities for guests, including a swimming pool, billiards, table-tennis, bicycles and much help on the places worth visiting in the area. (The château is not considered suitable for children under 15.) A first-class table d'hôte is provided on reservation. It is served in the spacious dining room which, like the rest of the château, has an atmosphere of gracious, cosmopolitan living.

34 CHATEAU DE NANTILLY H

♥ ♥ ★ ★

Nantilly, 70100 Gray, Haute-Saône.
Tel: 84 65 20 12
Telex: 362 888 F
Propr: M. Heinz & Mme Simone Magel
Open: All year

Restaurant: Closed Sun evening & Mon
Chef: M. Heinz Magel
Lunch: 1200 - 1400
Dinner: 1930 - 2200
Prix fixe: Menus at A & B
    A la carte available
Demi-pension   C-F

Seminars: max. 30
Groups: max. 30
Credit cards:
    American Express
    Diners Club
    Eurocard
    Visa
English & German spoken

Twin with bath	7	B-D
Double with bath	10	B-C
Suites (max. 3)	2	D-E
Total rooms:	19	

No lift

Tennis court
Swimming pool

Inter. Leading Association

48km north-east of Dijon. From there, take the D70 towards Gray. After 42km, just after passing through the village of Mantocke, turn left on the D269 to Nantilly. (If you miss the road, there are a couple of other left turnings before entering Gray.) **Airport:** *Dijon (50km)* **Station:** *Dijon (48km)*

This small, attractive château, set in ten acres of landscaped parkland, was built in 1830. The well-proportioned front has neat dormer windows in the grey-tiled roof. The central section is crowned with an elaborate stone pediment. Above the front door is a small balcony with a wrought-iron surround. In the downstairs rooms, there is some remarkable, intricate painted wooden panelling on the walls and matching, painted moulding on the ceilings. In the bar and reception area, there are wood-block floors laid in an intricate pattern. A staircase with a carved wooden ballustrade leads to the comfortable bedrooms with their immaculate bathrooms.

Heinz and Simone Magel took over the hotel at the beginning of 1988 and have redecorated throughout. They are extremely helpful and friendly patrons. Heinz is also the chef and has acquired a sound reputation for his cuisine which uses much fresh produce from the estate. There are two well-furnished dining rooms and a bar. Outside, for the use of guests, there's a swimming pool and a tennis court.

35 CHATEAU DE RIGNY H

♥ ★ ★
Rigny, 70101 Gray, Haute-
   Saône.
Tel: 84 65 25 01
Telex: 362 926 F
Propr: M. Jacques Maupin
Open: 1 Feb - 6 Jan

Twin with bath   13 B-C
Double with bath   11 B-C
   Total rooms: 24
(Rooms in château & annexe)

No lift. 4 ground-floor
   rooms.

Restaurant: Open every day
Lunch: 1200 - 1400
Dinner: 1900 - 2100
Prix fixe: Menus at A & B
   A la carte available
Chef: M. Jacques Maupin
Specialities: *Panaché de la
   mer au beurre de sauternes;
   Persillé de lapin au vinaigre
   de lavande; Cassolette
   d'escargots au beurre de
   poivron rouge; Noisettes
   d'agneau à l'essence de
   truffe.*

Seminars max. 30
Groups: max. 30
Credit cards:
   American Express
   Diners Club
   Eurocard
   Visa
English & Italian spoken

Swimming pool
Tennis court
Horse riding 4km

Relais du Silence, Châteaux
   et Demeures de Tradition

*54km north-east of Dijon. From there, take the D70 through Gray. Just afterwards, on the
outskirts of the town, turn right onto the D2 to Rigny.* **Airport:** *Dijon (60km)* **Station:**
Gray (5km) or Dijon (54km)

On the gateway of this seventeenth-century château is an inscription, dated 1789,
stating that, because of his loyalty, Rigny need not pay dues to the king. A
desperate revolutionary tried unsuccessfully to erase this testimonial of royal
largesse. Through the gates are verdant, peaceful grounds and a river where ducks
and swans swim contentedly. It is such an idyllic scene that the visitor is
unprepared for the exuberant, baroque style of the entrance hall. The walls are
painted a vibrant crimson and decorated with grinning boars' heads. There are two
heavily-carved galleries and oak panelling. On top of the massive overmantle
above the elaborate wooden fireplace is a life-size model of a woman imprisoned
between the carrying-poles of a sedan chair. Although not quite so outrageous, the
bedrooms in the château are similar in style and impact. One has burnt orange
walls, gold and white painted panelling, heavily-patterned gold and white draped

bed-hangings and glittering gold curtains. A parquet floor and brass chandelier add the finishing touches. The bedrooms in the annexe are newer and less eye-catching.

In comparison to the rest of the hotel, the two dining rooms seem agreeably sombre - one is decorated in rose tones, the other in soft blues. The cuisine of Jacques Maupin, the owner and chef, is good and the menus always include interesting, original dishes. The welcome is warm and the service is efficient.

36 CHATEAU DE GILLY H

♥ ♥ ★ ★

Gilly-les-Cîteaux, 21640
  Vougeot, Côte-d'Or.
Tel: 80 62 89 98
Telex: 351 467 F
Fax: 80 62 82 34
Propr: M. René Traversac,
  Grandes Etapes Francais
Direc: M. Jean-Louis
  Bottigliero
Open 5 March - 5 Jan

Twin with bath	16 C-G
Double with bath	16 C-G
Apartments	7 G-I
Total rooms:	39
(Further rooms being added)	

Restaurant: Open daily
Chef: M. Louis
  Schwendenman
Lunch: 1215 - 1430
Dinner: 1915 - 2130
Prix fixe: Menus at B & C
  A la carte available

Seminars: max. 80
Groups: max. 40
Receptions: max. 100
Credit cards:
  Visa
English & German
  spoken

Tennis courts

5km north of the Nuits-Saint-Georges exit from the A31 and 20km south of Dijon. From Dijon, take the N74 towards Beaune. After 19km, at Vougeot, turn left onto the D25 to Gilly-les-Cîteaux. The château is in the village to the right. **Airport:** *Dijon (17km)* **Station:** *Dijon (20km)*

Opened in 1988, this is the latest of René Traversac's superb châteaux-hotels. Set amidst some of France's most famous vineyards, Gilly is an ancient religious settlement, having been given to Saint Germain des Prés in the sixth century. Later, a Cistercian abbot's palace was built there in the late thirteenth century, when the surviving vaulted cellars were constructed to store the wine from the abbot's extensive vineyards. Most of the present complex of buildings, covering a hundred square metres and surrounded by a moat, was erected around 1625. The heavily beamed ceilings in many of the upper rooms were richly painted with intricate patterns. At the same time, a garden was laid with flower-beds, fountains and fruit-trees that became so famous it was visited by Louis XIV. During the eighteenth century, oak panelling was added to many of the ground-floor rooms.

  Almost everything at Gilly, including the interior and the gardens, had fallen into a dire state of decay when René Traversac acquired it early in 1988. With his renowned enthusiasm and dedication he set about the complex task of establishing a first class hotel while still retaining as much as possible of the features and character of the ancient buildings. As we were fortunate enough to be shown round by him, we were able to appreciate the enormity of the work that René Traversac - the saviour of so many of France's historical buildings - had undertaken.

To form a long, unbroken facade, the original wing was united with the old stable-block by building a central turreted section. Housing the reception area and the bar, it blends in so well with the rest of the buildings that already many people have assumed it is the oldest part of Château de Gilly. That isn't surprising, because the walls are constructed with vast stone blocks, there are thick wooden beams on the ceiling and suitable fittings throughout. Even the front of the bar is made from an eighteenth-century, thick wooden door. When the floor of the original storeroom was lowered to its original level, water began to seep in and so the moat was drained and grassed over. The large, vaulted area was then converted into an elegant dining room, connected to the main building by an underground walkway and a stone staircase. Near to this is another flight of stairs, leading up to the bright, delightful breakfast-room, with its original painted beams.

René Traversac has designed the interior to accommodate most satisfactorily the elegant bedrooms and their superbly equipped, marble-tiled bathrooms. All are decorated differently and vary in size, but all are superb. Best of all are the suites. The one we stayed in had the additional luxury of its own verandah and stone staircase leading down to the formal French garden, which like so much at Gilly, has had to be totally restored.

Work will continue until 1991. Additional rooms and suites are under construction. But already Château de Gilly is a delightful and extremely comfortable place to stay - a most welcome addition to the list of France's distinguished château-hotels.

37 CHATEAU DE LONGECOURT PG

♛ ♛ ♛ ★

Longecourt-en-Plaine, 21110
  Genlis, Côte-d'Or.
Tel: 80 39 88 76
Propr: Comtesse Bertrand de
  Saint-Seine
Open: All year

No lift. 1 ground-floor room.

Twin with shower	1 C
Twin with bath	2 D
Double bath	1 D
(inc. breakfast)	
Total rooms:	4
Table d'hôte on request	B
Demi-pension	E

Groups: max. 8
No credit cards
A little English spoken

Tennis court 800m
Swimming pool 8km
Golf course 30km

Châteaux Accueil

15km south of Dijon. From there, take the D968 to Longecourt-en-Plaine. In the village, take the second left. The château is straight ahead, opposite the church. **Airport:** *Dijon (17km)* **Station:** *Longecourt-en-Plaine or Dijon*

Although in the village, the château has ninety acres of parkland, surrounded by a wall and bordered by the Burgundy Canal. Not surprisingly, the woodland is a popular sanctuary for a great variety of birds. The original building on the site was constructed, in the thirteenth century, as a fortified house on piles for the Duke of Burgundy. During the sixteenth century, this simple structure was transformed into a manor house. During the following century, the family of the present proprietor acquired the property. In the eighteenth century, Nicolas Lenoir, known as 'The Roman', considerably embellished the house in the neo-classic Italian style.

Surrounded by a moat, the château forms a square. At each corner is a circular tower topped with a pointed tiled roof. The exterior is highly decorative with patterned red bricks and crumbling, carved white stone. To the left of the entrance is one of the oldest parts of the house - the chapel with its many original features, including unusual picture floor-tiles. The interior of the main château is delightful and reflects the fact that this has been the home of the same family for over three hundred years. Downstairs is a vast, bright reception room, with large windows overlooking the moat and parkland. At the end of the long corridor, a curved flight of stone steps leads to the impressive landing, hung with portraits of ancestors and

---

other French nobles. Leading off this, in the centre, is an amazing salon - the walls and ceiling heavily embellished with gilt rococo decorations. There are gigantic mirrors and crystal chandeliers. The bedrooms, though simple, are pleasing and comfortable. The bathrooms are excellent. Although she speaks only a little English, Comtesse Bernard de Saint-Seine is very helpful and gracious. The table d'hôte is very good indeed. Staying at Longecourt provides an ideal opportunity to share in the authentic life of an individual and a stylish French château.

38 HOTEL CHATEAU DE LA BERCHERE H

	Twin with bath	6 B	Credit cards:
Boncourt-le-Bois, 21700	Double with shower	5 B	Eurocard
Nuits-Saint-Georges, Côte-	Double with bath	2 B	Visa
d'Or	Total rooms:	13	English & German spoken
Tel: 80 61 01 40	No lift. 4 ground-floor		
Propr: M.J.C. Massart	rooms.		Tennis court 2km
Open: 1 March - 18 Jan			
	No restaurant.		

2km east of Nuits-Saint-Georges. 2km north of its exit on Autoroute 31, from which turn right at the first roundabout (the town is straight on). Take the first left and the château is 500m on the left. **Airport:** *Dijon (22km)* **Station:** *Nuits-Saint-Georges (2km)*

In the middle of the fifteenth century, a simple manor house was built for the Legouz family at the domaine de la Berchère. During the next couple of hundred years, the family's fortunes improved and the house was transformed into a magnificent château between 1597 and 1644 by Jean Baptiste Legouz and his son, Pierre, who became the President of the parliament of Burgundy. The family continued to own the property until 1738, when it was sold and some restoration work was undertaken. After the Revolution, the château was owned by a variety of people and the fabric slowly deteriorated. In 1920, Château de la Berchère passed into the family of the present proprietor.

Occupying three sides of a central courtyard, the exterior of the building is beautiful. The main wing, however, has badly deteriorated and is at present but a ruin. Recently, one of the other wings has been modernised and the interior has been divided into small, anonymous but comfortable, motel-like bedrooms with their own small bathrooms. All have delightful views of the surrounding area. Being so close to the autoroute, the château provides an easy and inexpensive stopping-off place in one of France's most-famous wine-growing areas.

---

39 CHATEAU DE SAULON LA RUE

H

♥ ★

Route de Seurre, Saulon-la-Rue, 21910 Saulon-la-Chapelle, Côte-d'Or.
Tel: 80 36 61 10
Telex: 350 571 F
Propr: Comtesse d'Oillianson
Direc: Mme Catherine Perrette
Open: All year

Single with bath	3 B
Single with shared w.c.	2 B
Twin with bath	9 B
Double with bath	19 B
Total rooms:	33

Restaurant: Open every day
Lunch: 1230 - 1500
Dinner: 1900 - 2200
Prix fixe: Menus at A & B
    A la carte available
Speciality: *Cuisine bourguignon.*
Seminars: max. 100
Groups: max. 45
Receptions: max. 100

No lift. 2 ground-floor rooms.
(7 rooms in an annexe)

Credit cards
    American Express
    Diners Club
    Visa
English, German & Italian spoken

Fishing
Tennis court
Horse riding 8km
Swimming pool 10km

Châteaux Hôtels Indép.
La Castellerie

10km south of Dijon. From there, take the D986. After 5km, just after the airport, fork right onto the D996. The château is in Saulon-la-Rue on the left. **Airport:** *Dijon (5km)* **Station:** *Dijon (10km)*

Although just off a busy main-road, this vast, four-storeyed, white-stone château is most peaceful, being surrounded by a sixty-five acre wooded park through which a stream flows. The present house was built between 1832 and 1835. Sections of the earlier, sixteenth-century château were incorporated into the building. Recently, much renovation has converted the place into an inexpensive, popular hotel and restaurant. In the entrance hall, there is an ancient curved stone archway partially formed by the underneath of the stairs; on the floor are nineteenth-century black-and-white tiles. Next door, there is a small bar. The restaurant, which is in a separate building nearby, has a vaulted ceiling with rough plaster covering the original brick-work. Throughout the château, the modern furniture is plain and basic. The bedrooms are comfortable, although somewhat ordinary, with parquet floors and new, utility wardrobes, tables and chairs. But Saulon-la-Rue does not claim to be luxurious. It is an inexpensive hotel in a delightful setting close to Dijon.

♥ ♥
Guipy, 58420 Brinon-sur-
  Beuvron, Nièvre.
Tel: 86 29 01 26
Propr: Société Diane de
  Chanteloup
Open: All year

Double with bath   2 B

No lift

No restaurant

No credit cards
A little English spoken

· Equitation centre

Gîtes de France

56km north-east of Nevers. From there, take the D977 (towards Varzy). After 29km, just after passing through Prémery, turn right on the D977bis (towards Corbigny). After 22km, at Guipy, turn left onto the D135. After 3km, this meets the D5. Turn left and after 1km, turn left on the D274 to Chanteloup. Just before the village is the entrance to the château on the left. Ignore the sign saying that cars are forbidden (which applies to people visiting the pony club) and carry on up the long drive to the château. **Station:** *Corbigny (11.5km)*

So named since the Middle Ages, Chanteloup is a word derived from 'le champ des loups' - the countryside of wolves. Set among lawns on a hill-top overlooking the wooded valleys of the rivers Beuvron and Corneau, the site has long been occupied and the surviving château is an important historical and architectural monument. The central part was built during the sixteenth century to replace an earlier building of which all that remains are the vaulted caves and a dovecot. During the eighteenth century, a substantial north-east wing was added and the south tower was substantially restored. Further modifications were made during the nineteenth century when Chanteloup was much visited by socialites, especially during the brief rule of Louis XVIII. Later, in 1876, the owner, Charles-Martin de Chanteloup, built a gigantic underground reservoir and viaduct so the château and its fountains could be supplied with water under pressure.

Château de Chanteloup now belongs to the community and is used primarily as a cultural centre. (As a separate enterprise, there is a small equitation centre in part of the grounds.) Two chambres d'hôte are also available. Pleasantly furnished, both have bathrooms (with a very small bath), but only one has its own toilet.

Breakfast is served in a large dining room with a chandelier and large tapestry on the wall. There is a resident housekeeper, who is extremely pleasant and helpful. But, being neither a family home nor an hotel, the château has a somewhat anonymous air. It is, however, an unusual and inexpensive place to stay, set as it is among some extremely beautiful countryside.

41 CHATEAU DE LANTILLY PG

♛ ♛ ♛ ★
Lantilly, 58800 Corbigny,
  Nièvre.
Tel: 86 20 01 22
Propr: Mme Gisèle Ramillon
Open: All year

Twin with bath	6 B-C
Double with bath	3 B-C
(inc. breakfast)	
Total rooms:	9
No lift	

Table d'hôte on
  reservation A
Lunch: 1230 - 1330
Dinner: 1930 - 2030
Specialities: *Brochet aux
  ecrevisses; Cassolette
  d'escargots en robe
  morvandelle; Pintade
  (guinea-fowl) au Marc de
  Bourgogne.*
Demi-pension B

Seminars: max. 30
Groups: max. 20
No credit cards
English & German spoken

Equitation centre
Swimming pool
Fishing
Tennis courts 3.5km

Châteaux et Demeures de
Tradition, Les Etapes
François Coeur

*28km south of Vezelay. From there, take the D958 to Corbigny. Carry straight on through
the town onto the D285, a minor-road leading to Mouron-sur-Yonne. After 3km, turn left
onto a narrow road. The château is on the right after 600m.* **Station:** *Corbigny (4km)*

First built in the thirteenth century on the site of a Roman villa, the château was
considerably extended during the seventeenth century. Its two surviving wings are
totally surrounded by a wide moat. It is an extraordinary place. Little seems to have
changed over the centuries. The exterior is almost untouched. Inside, those
additions have been made that were necessary to make the bedrooms suitable as
chambres d'hôte, but the solutions are sometimes bizarre - in the bedrooms
furnished with astonishing antiques there are bathrooms behind curtains, in
alcoves, under eves with mini-baths and mobile bidets. The place will not suit

those who are expecting modern hotel amenities, but for those wishing to stay in a rural French home, situated in an ancient and little changed castle, it is ideal. Mme Gisèle Ramillon is exceptionally kind, generous and helpful, doing everything she can to make her guests feel at home - though she speaks no English. There is a large swimming pool in the delightful garden and a billiard room for the use of guests. Best of all is the food, served in the extraordinary dining room with its high, beamed ceilings. There is a choice of dishes as large as in many posh restaurants. A typical dinner has escargot, trout baked with hazel-nuts, rabbit with truffles, salad, vegetables, and a delicious meringue with strawberries and Cassis - and all for a price less than is often demanded for a main course. There is also an adequate wine-list, including five champagnes.

42 CHATEAU DE LESVAULT PG

🛡 ★ ★ ♈

Onlay, 58370 Villapourcon,
   Nièvre.
Tel: 86 84 32 91
Propr: Mme Berit 'Bibbi' Lee
Open: All year

No lift

Doubles with bath	6 C
Double with shared bath	4 B
(inc. breakfast)	
Total rooms:	10

Table d'hôte on res. A
Dinner: 2000
Chef: M. David de Bruin
Demi-pension B

Seminars: max. 30
Groups: max. 16
Credit cards:
   American Express
   Visa
English, German, Italian,
   Spanish & Norwegian
   spoken

Gîtes de France

65km east of Nevers. From there, take the D978. After 47km, and shortly after Tamnay-en-Bazois, turn right onto the D985, through Moulins-Engilbert. 5.4km later, the château is on the left, before the village of Onlay. **Airport:** *Nevers (67km)* **Station:** *Nevers (65km)*

This delightful château, built in 1860, is not only a chambre d'hôte of the highest standard but also a flourishing contemporary art and cultural centre. With a Norwegian director and an American chef, it is an international community, attracting guests from all over the world. The château has been completely redecorated and delightfully furnished in a non-fussy, elegant style. The bedrooms are spacious and pleasing and the bathrooms are excellent. The dining room is on the lower ground floor. It's a simple room, but full of atmosphere, with stone-flag floors and an enormous fireplace. Guests sit around a long refectory table. Most evening meals are highly animated affairs, full of lively conversation and laughter. The food is excellent and the menus cosmopolitan. One night we were there, we ate a delicious Chinese meal cooked in the kitchen next-door. There was also a splendid selection of wines.

There is a well-stocked library and exhibitions of the latest works by an international group of artists. Arrangements can be made for cultural visits and full-scale guided-tours can be organised by experts. Many sporting activities are available in the area. Bibbi Lee is a witty and amiable hostess who really makes her guests feel at home, providing, for example, informative notes on the region. And

Top: **Château de Vault-de-Lugny** (55) Yonne (Burgundy)
Bottom: **Château de la Vigne** (61) Cantal (Auvergne)

Château de Divonne (67) Ain (Rhone-Alpes)

the beautiful surrounding countryside, with its rolling green hills and dense forests, is little known and well worth exploring — bicycles are available for hire. From November to March, rooms in the château may be booked by writers for a month at a time. Full board is provided and the cost is very reasonable. It's a perfect place for a writers' retreat. Strongly recommended.

43 CHATEAU DE MIMONT PG

♛ ★ ★ ★	Double with bath 8 B-C	Credit cards:
58320 Pouges-les-Eaux,	Suite (max. 4) 1 D	Visa
Nièvre.		English spoken
Tel: 86 68 81 44	No restaurant	
Proprs: M. & Mme Alasnier-		Swimming pool
Prégermain	Seminars: max. 30	Tennis court
Open: All year (reservation	Groups: max 15	Horse riding 4km
only in winter)	Receptions: max. 100	
		Château Accueil
No lift		Gîtes de France

20km north of Nevers. From there, take the N7 to Pouges-les-Eaux. Turn right onto the D8 and shortly afterwards turn left onto a minor road to Satinges. Carrying on through the village, the road winds up a hill. The château is a further 1km on the left. **Airport:** *Nevers (23km)* **Station:** *Pouges-les-Eaux (4km)*

Archaeologists have discovered at Mimont some dolmen - believed to be Druid tombs or monuments — and sacrificial stones. The religious links with the site continued. In the eleventh century, an abbey was built there, but it was destroyed during the Revolution. All that now remains is a small stone statue of a monk and part of a wall. At the beginning of the nineteenth century, the present château was constructed on the abbey's foundations. The impressive building consists of two large wings standing at right angles to embrace a courtyard and rectangular formal garden.

From as early as the twelfth century, Mimont has been a centre for Chasse à Courre — hunting wild boar and stag on horseback in the surrounding forest. The tradition is continued by the present owner, whose family acquired the château after the Second World War. Hunting takes place from November to March. The motto of Château de Mimont is 'Au bois comme à table', 'In the woods as though at the table'.

Since 1962, Mimont has been a château-hotel. Most of the furniture dates from the eighteenth or early nineteenth centuries. In the lounge, there is a Charles X

---

suite and on the floor is Louis XIV parquet. Leading up from the entrance is a pink marble staircase. Our bedroom was enormous, with a vast marble fireplace and interesting antique furniture and paintings. A flight of marble stairs led down to the magnificent bathroom, which has a huge double porcelain washbasin and matching table. Although not all as large, the other bedrooms are extremely well furnished and comfortable. Breakfast is served in the bedrooms on china monogrammed with a boar's head and the château's motto.

Downstairs, there is an enormous room used for weddings and other celebrations. So, if you're looking for the peace and quiet normally found at Mimont, it's best to avoid Saturday evenings — though, as travellers in France soon discover, French weddings are jolly occasions to which everybody seems to be cordially invited. Close to the château, in the seventy-acre grounds, are a swimming pool and a tennis court.

44 MANOIR DE VALOTTE PG

♥ ♥
Valotte, 58270 Saint-Benin
  d'Azy, Nièvre.
Tel: 86 58 43 83
Propr: Princess M.D. de
  Croy
Open: All year

No lift

Double with bath   5 B
Double with shared w.c.   2 B
  Total rooms: 7
(Breakfast served only on
  first morning)

No restaurant

No credit cards

English & German spoken

Swimming pool 3km
Horse riding 4km
Golf course 20km

22km east of Nevers. From there, take the D978 (towards Besançon). After 20km, turn right into the village of Saint-Benin d'Azy. Take the D172 (which has no markings) and not the D9 leading to La Machine and Decize. After 1.5km, turn right down a narrow road. The château is a further 500m on the left. **Airport:** *Nevers (20km)* **Station:** *Nevers (22km)*

Built as a fortified farm-house in the fifteenth century, Manoir de Valotte has been owned for many years by Princess M. D. de Croy, a member of one of France's oldest and most influential families. Until she retired, some years ago, she farmed the surrounding land, which is part of the family estate. (One of her sisters lives, a kilometre away, in the huge family château just outside Saint-Benin d'Azy.) There is much about Manoir de Valotte that is unconventional. When we arrived, preparations were well underway for the annual rock festival that the princess holds in one of her fields during the first weekend in June. Musicians were encamped in the old stables, which also include a small sound studio, where Julian Lennon recorded his first album. We were directed to the large, jumbled sitting-room at the rear of the house, where we found the princess. She informed us that the door had to be left open so that the birds nesting in the beams of the room could fly in and out. There were several other pets in the room, including a dog with blue eyes. We later discovered that the princess has closed off the upper part of the large square tower at the front of the house, because owls nest there.

The bedrooms are filled with interesting bric-a-brac and furnished in a strange assortment of antique and modern furniture. The bathrooms are basic. Amid the rafters of the house, there is a vast yet attractive lounge of a hundred square metres, with a couple of sofa beds and a fire-place. This is one of three areas in the house equipped with a kitchen so that guests can prepare their own meals. The place may not be to everyone's taste, but it is much favoured by young people, especially from Holland and Germany.

45 CHATEAU LA FREDIERE PG

♥ ♥ ★

Ceron, 71110 Marcigny, Saône-et-Loire.	Twin with shower	3 B
	Twin with bath	3 A-C
Tel: 85 25 19 67	Double with shower	1 B
Propr: Mme Edith Charlier	Double with bath	3 A-C
Open: 11 Jan - 19 Dec	Total rooms	10

Twin with shower 3 B   Seminars: max 10
Twin with bath 3 A-C   Groups: max. 20
Double with shower 1 B   No credit cards
Double with bath 3 A-C   English & German spoken
Total rooms 10
(6 rooms in château & 4 in   Practice golf
the club house)   Tennis courts
Table d'hôte (on
reservation) in club   Château Accueil
house A   Inter. Leading Assocation

Ceron, 71110 Marcigny,
Saône-et-Loire.
Tel: 85 25 19 67
Propr: Mme Edith Charlier
Open: 11 Jan - 19 Dec

No lift

36km north of Roanne. From there, take the D982. After 30km, at Marcigny, turn left onto the D990. At Les Roussins, 4km further, turn right to Cèron. In the village, turn right, opposite the church. At the next junction, take the left fork. The château is a little further on the right. **Airport:** *Roanne (38km)* **Station:** *Marcigny (7km)*

Set in a beautiful and peaceful park, this nineteenth-century château is charming. Sturdy and square, it has a circular, tile-covered tower at each corner of its cream walls with white stone decorations around each window. The ground-floor rooms have polished parquet floors, white-painted wood panelling and pleasant decorations. The elegant period furniture, the paintings on the walls, the fire burning in the grate and the interesting objects displayed in every room create a relaxed and appealing atmosphere. Breakfast is served either in the attractive dining room or on the terrace overlooking the tree-shaded garden. The bedrooms are comfortable and well furnished, mostly with period furniture. The six rooms in the château have been given appropriate names, such as Chambre Empire, Chambre aux Cyclamens or Chambre de la Tour. Although comfortable, the four bedrooms in the golf club house are much more utilitarian and considerably cheaper. Situated close to the Loire, Château La Fredière provides a peaceful and pleasant place to stay. Madame Charlier, the owner, is kind and helpful. The 9-hole golf-course and putting-green she has introduced are amenities much appreciated by many guests.

46 HOSTELLERIE DU CHATEAU DE BELLECROIX H

♥ ♥ ★ ★
71150 Chagny, Saône-et-
  Loire.
Tel: 85 87 13 86
Fax: 85 91 28 62
Propr: Mme Evelyne Gautier
Open: 1 Feb - 20 Dec.
  Closed every Wed

Twin with shower	3 C
Twin with bath	12 C-D
Double with bath	4 C-D
Total rooms:	19

No lift. 2 ground-floor
Restaurant: Closed Wed
Chef: M Jean-Francois Barbier
Lunch: 1200 - 1400
Dinner: 1930 - 2100
Prix fixe: Menus at A
  A la carte available
Specialities: *Terrine de foie
gras de canard fait maison;
Filet de boeuf à la moelle
et au xérès; Feuilleté de
poires sauce caramel.*
Demi-pension (3 days+) C

Seminars: max. 70
Groups: max. 30
Credit cards:
  American Express
  Diners Club
  Mastercard
  Visa
English & Spanish spoken
Swimming pool
Tennis court 1km
Golf course 10 km
Châteaux Hôtels Indép.
Relais du Silence

*16km north-west of Chalon-sur-Saône and the Chalon nord exit from Autoroute 6. Take the
N6 towards Chagny. After 16km, just before reaching Chagny, turn right to Bellecroix.*
Airport: *Autun (43km)* **Station:** *Chalon or Beaune (16km)*

This vine-clad château with its two round towers topped by steep turrets started
life in 1199 as a Commanderie for the Knights of Saint John. Although much
remodelled during the eighteenth century, some of the ancient building survives,
due mainly, one suspects, to the fact that the original walls were two metres thick.
In the five-acre park, there is a fifteenth century cross with the Virgin on one side,
and Christ with a cross of Malta in his halo on the other.

During the last decade, Mme Gauthier has converted the château into a pleasant
and comfortable hotel. On entering Bellecroix, there is a vast wood-panelled room
with a huge stone fireplace that is both the reception area and the dining room.
Two smaller, more intimate dining areas are in the base of the round towers. Four
of the bedrooms are also in the towers and they are reached by means of a splendid
spiral staircase. The three most expensive bedrooms and a magnificent lounge are
in another building, behind the château. All the bedrooms are well furnished,
mainly with antiques, including canopied beds. With a sound reputation for the
quality of its cuisine, Château de Bellecroix is an attractive place to stay.

47 CHATEAU DE FLEURVILLE H

🛡 ★
71260 Fleurville, Saône-et-
  Loire.
Tel: 85 33 12 17
Propr: M. Naudin
Open: 20 Dec - 15 Oct,
  weekends only in Feb

Twin with bath   8 B
Double with bath   6 B
  Total rooms: 14
Apartment: 1

No lift. 2 ground-floor
  rooms

Restaurant: Closed Mon
  lunch
Lunch: 1200 - 1315
Dinner: 1930 - 2100
Chef: M. Naudin
Prix fixe: Menus at A & B
  A la carte available
Specialities: *Quenelles de
  fromage de chèvre aux fines
  herbes; Filet de truite
  rose à la crème d'estragon;
  Pigeon de Bresse en compote.*
Demi-pension (3 days+) C

Seminars: max. 50
Groups: max. 30
Receptions: max. 60
Credit cards:
  American Express
  Diners Club
  Visa
English & German spoken

Swimming pool
Tennis court 1km
Horse riding 3km
Golf course 15km

Châteaux Hôtels Indép.

North of the Mâcon nord exit from Autouroute 6 and 17km north of Mâcon. From there, take the N6 to Fleurville. The château is on the left. **Airport:** *Mâcon (19km)* **Station:** *Mâcon (17km)*

This is definitely not a swanky place, but it does have some nice features. Built between the sixteenth and the eighteenth centuries, it once belonged to Princess de Talleyrand. Comtesse de Segur wrote books there. It has a pretty exterior, with a thin round tower. There is a small park; a magnolia tree shades the terrace. For over twenty-five years, it has been a hotel. The dining rooms are pleasant, with simple furniture, plain walls and heavily-beamed ceilings. There are other rooms, however, where the decoration and furnishings are less attractive. The bedrooms, although comfortable, are small and basic. The food and wine are good and reasonably priced. Although very close to the N6, it is surprisingly peaceful and makes a convenient stopping-off point while touring the Burgundy wine area.

48 CHATEAU D'IGE H

ʊ ʊ ★ ★
Ige. 71960 Pierreclos, Saône-et-Loire.
Tel: 85 33 33 99
Telex: 351 915 F
Fax: 85 33 41 41
Propr: M. Henri Jadot
Open: 1 March - 15 Nov

Double with bath	6 B-C
Suites	6 D
Total rooms:	12

No lift

Restaurant: Open daily
Lunch: 1200 - 1330
Dinner: 1930 - 2100
Prix fixe: Menus at A & B
  A la carte available

Seminars: max. 25
Groups: max. 30
Receptions: max. 100

Credit cards:
  American Express
  Diners Card
  Eurocard
  Visa
English, German & Italian
  spoken
Swimming pool 3km
Tennis courts 3km
Golf course 12km

Relais & Châteaux

West of the Mâcon nord exit from Autoroute 6. 14km north-west of Mâcon. From there, take the N79 towards Cluny. After 11km, at La Roche-Vineuse, turn right on the D85 to Ige. **Airport:** *Mâcon (12km)* **Station:** *Mâcon (14km)*

Built in 1235, this pretty old stone castle is adorned with russet vine-leaves and Russian vines. Once the home of feudal barons, its owners fled during the French Revolution. From that time, it stood empty until, in the mid 1960s, Henri Jadot - with great patience and skill - restored and converted the château into a most agreeable hotel. There are two dining rooms - both have beamed ceilings, but the smaller of the two is most impressive, with a massive stone fireplace, stone walls, polished tiled floors and a long refectory table. All the bedrooms are elegantly furnished and decorated with commendable restraint. The best are the suites which, being in the tower, are circular. Each has a luxurious bathroom and is reached by a spiral staircase. The food is good - straightforward and enjoyable, including escargot raised in the garden and trout from the château's own holding-pond. The service is friendly and efficient. Henri Jadot is a most welcoming host.

---

49 CHATEAU DE POUJUX PG

🛡🛡 ★ ★
Saint-Aubin-en-Charollais,
71430 Palinges, Saône-et-
Loire.
Tel: 85 70 43 64
Propr: M. & Mme Christian
Céaly-Oberli
Open: All year

No lift. 1 room & suite on
ground-floor.

Single with bath	2 B
Twin with shower	2 C
Twin with bath	4 C
Double with bath	1 C
Suite (max. 4)	1 E
Total rooms:	10 E
Table d'hôte on reservation	A
Demi pension (6 days+)	B

Seminars: max. 25
Groups: max. 15
No credit cards
English, German & Dutch
spoken

Horse-breeding centre

Châteaux Accueil

57km west of Mâcon. From there, take the N79 (direction Nevers & Moulins). After 45km, do not take the Charolles by-pass, but enter the town and turn right onto the D985. After 7.5km, turn left to Saint-Aubin-en-Charollais. **Station:** *Paray-le-Monial (22km)*

Château de Poujux now stands where once there was a Roman villa. In the centuries between, many other buildings were erected and demolished. The present, beautifully proportioned manor-house was built in the eighteenth century. Looking almost like an elaborate doll's house, with its clean lines and neatly painted shutters, it stands amid neatly clipped lawns and hedges. For almost a century, Poujux has been a stud where many of the country's top racing-horses have been bred. The present owners continue that tradition and the racing colours of Poujux - gold and black - are seen at the world's best race-courses. M. and Mme Céaly-Oberli communicate their passion for horse-racing and horse-breeding most poetically in French. A translation does not do their words justice, but they say: 'If at Poujux you speak of horses, then the breeze is stilled, the rain ceases to fall, and you enter into a new universe, a passionate world where the stride of a foal galloping through the grass glittering with the dew of early morning will make you understand the basis of the life of your hosts - a life coloured with black and gold, but a meaningful life.'

In 1988, the châteaux was completely renovated and the bedrooms decorated and equipped to a high standard. A delightful place - especially for horse-lovers.

50 CHATEAU DE SAINT-GERMAIN-DU-PLAIN PG

♥ ♥ ★ ★
71370 Saint-Germain-du-
  Plain, Saône-et-Loire.
Tel: 85 47 40 31, 85 47 40 31
Proprs: M. & Mme Eric
  Villard
Open: All year

Twin with bath	3 D
Double with bath	3 D
Suites (max. 3)	2 F
Total rooms:	8
No lift	

Table d'hôte on reservation.
  (Obligatory on day of
  arrival)
Chef: M. Eric Villard
Cuisine régionale allégée

Credit cards:
  American Express
  Diners Club
  Visa
English, German & Italian
  spoken

Fishing 2km
Horse riding 2km
Golf course 15km
Swimming pool 15km
Ballooning

Château Accueil
Inter. Leading Association
La Castellerie

12km south-east of Chalon-sur-Saône (and Autoroute 6). Take the N73. After 2km, at Saint-Marcel, turn right onto the D978 to Saint-Germain. **Airport:** *Chalon (14km)* **Station:** *Chalon (12km)*

At the beginning of the French Revolution, the château then existing at Saint-Germain-du-Plain was confiscated by the state. It was sold in 1827 to a local family whose only child, Marie-Louise, married Eugène Henry de Verchère. During the next twenty years, they pulled down the original and built a new château incorporating the old cellars and using some of the antique stones in the staircase. The mid-nineteenth century was not the golden age of château design — the exteriors of the Napoleonic style are over-decorated and the interiors too dark. Saint-Germain-du-Plain is better than most, although it still has the fussy facade of red brick and ornamental white stone that seems overdressed amidst the serenity of a large wooded park. The Verchère family continued to own the property until 1985, when the last of the line was, at the age of 86, tragically drowned in the garden pond.

Shortly afterwards, the château with its twelve-acre park containing many ancient trees was bought by Eric and Claire Villard, who hail from Switzerland. Over the next twelve months and at considerable expense, they meticulously restored the fabric and refurbished it with antiques, including four-poster beds in the very comfortable bedrooms, which have excellent bathrooms. For many guests, the high-spot of their stay is the evening meal, which is seen as being very much a social occasion hosted by M. and Mme Villard. Originally an architect, Eric Villard has a passionate interest in cooking and, as the chef, he produces refreshingly simple but extremely tasty dishes, such as *marinade de volaille de Bresse* and *mignon de porc au cumin*. The wine cellar is stocked with a large range of Burgundies.

Many special attractions are arranged for guests at the château. There are fixed-price weekends, a four-day golfing stay, a nine-nine holiday combining relaxation and golf, a cuisine-sampling course conducted by Georges Tertuiset and a costumed 1900 weekend. Guests can hire a helicopter, one of Eric Villard's collection of antique cars, or a hot-air balloon. Excursions can also be arranged to local tourist spots.

Guests are accepted only if a reservation has been made and a 30 per cent deposit paid. Dinner on the day of arrival is mandatory.

51 LE PARC DES MARÉCHAUX H

ᗊ ★

6 Avenue Foch, 89000
   Auxere, Yonne.
Tel: 85 51 43 77
Propr: Mme Espérance Hervé
Open: All year

Lift. 3 ground-floor rooms.

Twin with bath   20 B
Suites (max. 3)   4 B
   Total rooms: 24

No restaurant

Seminars: max. 12
Groups: max. 40

Credit cards:
   American Express
   Eurocard
   Visa
English & Spanish spoken

La Castellerie

In Auxerre. The hotel is to the west of the city, just off the ringroad. If arriving from Paris (via the A6), you approach the city on the N6, which becomes Avenue Charles de Gaulle. At the ringroad, turn right (into Boulevard Vauban). The third main exit on the right is Avenue Foch. The hotel is almost immediately on the right. **Airport:** *Auxerre (7km)* **Station:** *Auxerre (1km)*

This town house with its white louvered shutters was built during the reign of Napoleon III. The front of the building is very close to the road, but at the back there is a most agreeable park filled with ancient trees - a most tranquil spot in what is quite a large town. Le Parc des Maréchaux is definitely not a luxury hotel, but its very feminine decor is most agreeable. Refreshingly, the colours mainly used are white, cream and warm autumnal shades of terracotta. The reception hall, bar and breakfast room have painted half-panelling. The cream and white lounge has ornamental plaster borders on the walls. With its view across the park, it is a pleasant place in which to linger. Like all the public rooms, it has solid traditional furniture. There are pot plants and flowers throughout the hotel. There are prints on the walls, books on the shelves and china ornaments on the mantels above the fireplaces. Everywhere is immaculate, including the comfortable bedrooms with their period furniture and modern bathrooms. Although there is no restaurant at the hotel, there are many close by, including Le Jardin Gourmand, where the food is first-class. Le Parc des Maréchaux is a charming, unpretentious and inexpensive place to stay and Mme Espérance Hervé is a most helpful and courteous proprietor.

52 LE CASTEL H

★

89660 Mailly-le-Château, Yonne.
Tel: 86 40 43 06
Propr: M. & Mme Michel Breerette
Open: 15 March - 15 Nov

Twin with shower	2 B
Twin with bath	3 B
Double with shower	3 B
Double with bath	4 B
Total rooms:	12

No lift. 2 ground-floor rooms.

Restaurant: Closed Wed
Chef: M. Michel Breerette
Lunch: 1200 - 1330
Dinner: 1915 - 2030
Prix fixe: Menus at A & B
A la carte available
Specialities: *Escargots aux noisettes; Foie gras frais de canard maison et sa gelée au Porto; Pavé de charolais à la moutarde; Gratin de framboises et sa liqueur.*
Demi-pension   B

Seminars: max. 12
Groups: max. 20
Receptions: max. 45
Credit cards:
  Eurocard
  Visa
English & Spanish spoken

Tennis court 55m
Horse riding 7km

Relais du Silence
Gîtes de France

28.5km south of Auxerre. From there, take the D239 (towards Avallon). The road leads into the N6. Continue on this for a further 6km. Then turn right onto the D100. After 10.5km, continue on the D950 to Mailly-le-Château. The hotel is in the centre of the village, opposite the church. **Station:** *Mailly-la-Ville (4km)*

Directly opposite the village's splendid thirteenth-century church, this substantial house was built at the end of the last century. It has been a hotel and restaurant for many years. Facing the main square, the large central section of Le Castel has a much smaller wing set at right angles to it. These two parts of the house enclose a small terrace and garden where, in summer, breakfast and drinks are served beneath the shady lime trees. Le Castel is a simple, old-fashioned French country hotel, run by a charming family who provide good service and excellent food at a most reasonable price. The proprietor, Michel Breerette, has a high reputation in the area for his traditional cuisine and the two sections of the dining room are very busy. Our first meal there was at lunchtime - visits we had made to more luxurious châteaux had left us ill-prepared for the generosity of the portions. The bedrooms are basic, but comfortable. Four of the bedrooms do not have their own w.c.

53 CHATEAU DE PRUNOY PG

♥ ♥ ★ ★

Prunoy, 89120 Charny,
   Yonne.
Tel: 86 63 66 91, 86 63 67 91
Propr: Josée Roumilhac
Open: 5 March to 5 January

Twin with bath	4 B-C
Double with bath	9 B-C
Suite (max. 4)	1 D
Total rooms:	14

No lift. 3 ground-floor
   rooms.

Restaurant: Open daily
Chef: Josée Roumilhac
Lunch: 1230 - 1400
Dinner: 2000 - 2130
Prix fixe: Menus at A
Demi-pension (3 days+) B

Seminars: max. 18
Groups: max. 25
Receptions: max. 150

Credit cards:
   American Express
   Visa

Horse riding
Fishing
Tennis court
Practice golf

Châteaux Hôtels Indép.
Château Accueil, Les Etapes
François Coeur

23km west of Joigny (and 16km from exit on Autoroute 6). From Joigny, take the D943. At Villefranche - 10km after passing under the A6 - turn left onto the D18 to Prunoy. The château is on the right, just before entering the village. **Station:** *Joigny (23km)*

The original château at Prunoy was built in 1510. Apart from one circular tower, now used as a library, everything was razed to the ground in 1726 when the then owner, François Christophe de Lalive, a finance minister, ordered the construction of a new château. He created a beautiful and impressive building with the perfect symmetry of the classical eighteenth-century style. Two square towers are at either end of the main facade with its large shuttered windows. Next to the towers are two wings - one much smaller then the other, which is attached to the original Gothic tower. Among the subsequent occupants of the château was Jacques Raverat, who was educated in England and in the decade before the First World War became, with Rupert Brooke, a leader of the group of intellectuals Virginia Woolfe christened the 'Neo Pagans'. In 1926, Prunoy was acquired by the Roumilhac family. During the Second World War, the château was occupied by the Germans. By the late sixties, when Josée Roumilhac inherited the property, it was in a state of considerable decay. In 1981, she decided to live in the property, completely renovating it so that it could be opened to the public.

There is about Prunoy an informal, even scatty, air that can be very appealing. All the rooms have been refurbished and decorated with enthusiasm and a romantic, perhaps even theatrical, spirit. There are flowers everywhere - although some of them are artificial. The reception rooms are charming, with their heavily panelled walls. In one of the rooms, these have been varnished; in another they are painted blue and white. In both hang enormous glass chandeliers. All the bedrooms are very different and unusual. Furnished with some antiques, most are decorated in a dominant colour or style, reflected in the room's name - Bleue, Azur, 1900, Bambou and Coloniale, for example. In the somewhat tatty suite, there is a sauna, which can be used by guests when the suite is unoccupied. Our favourite bedroom is Rose, which has a most delightful bathroom. Also on the first floor is the library, situated in the old round tower. There is a polished, patterned wood-block floor and an interesting collection of books is stored in heavy wooden bookcases lining the wall.

Although the restaurant is rather folksy, the food is good and inexpensive. Wedding and confirmation receptions are held at the château on many Saturday nights. These can be somewhat noisy affairs, but around the house is a vast park of over 200 acres, designed by a student of Le Nôtre, which is exceptionally peaceful and relaxing. Not to everyone's taste, but we found it an agreeable place to stay.

54 HOSTELLERIE DU CHATEAU DE CLAIRIS H

♻ ★ ★

89150 Savigny-sur-Clairis.
Tel: 86 86 30 01
Propr: Mme E. Neyraval
Open: 8 Jan - 20 Dec

Twin with shower	5 B
Twin with bath	6 B
Double with shower	3 B
Double with bath	9 B
Total rooms:	23
No lift	

Restaurant: Open daily
Chef: M. Jean-Michel Kirche
Lunch: 1200 - 1330
Dinner: 2000 - 2100
Prix fixe: Menus at A & B
   A la carte available
Specialities: *Selon les
   marchés et les saisons;
   Savarin de saumon fumé; La
   tourte de rognons de veau aux
   moeilles.*
Demi-pension   C

Seminars: max. 50
Credit cards:
   American Express
   Diners Club, Visa
English spoken
Horse riding
16 tennis courts
Swimming pools
13-hole golf course

La Castellerie, Châteaux et
Demeures de Tradition

*21km south-west of Sens. Close to the Courteney exit from Autoroute 6. From there, turn
right onto the N60, towards Sens. Take the first left to Savigny-sur-Clairis and turn left
onto the D149. The château is less than 1km on the left.* **Station:** *Courtenay or Sens*

Surrounded by a 400-acre park, this château is now at the centre of a developing
and extremely popular sporting complex. There are 16 tennis courts, an Olympic-
size swimming pool, a horse-riding centre, jogging-course, golf course, sauna, sun-
lounge, and many other activities, including table-tennis room and playrooms. The
food is excellent and the bedrooms pleasant and well furnished. There is a
comfortable lounge with polished parquet floor, two compact dining rooms, a
spectacular entrance hall with a tiled floor and sweeping staircase and an adequate
bar. Eating or drinking on the terrace is delightful. Yet the costs of staying at this
château are very reasonable. So what's the catch? There really isn't one - although
on our arrival we found the reception staff unhelpful to the point of rudeness. The
château is a solid Lego-looking construction that was built in 1850 and given a more
antique appearance before the end of the century by a later owner. It's pleasant
enough in a rather clonky way. So for those more interested in outdoor sports or
a comfortable hotel than in château architecture, de Clairis has much to offer - and
they can always choose to stay in one of the modern studios built nearby.

55 CHATEAU DE VAULT-DE-LUGNY H

♨ ♨ ★ ★
Vault-de-Lugny, 89200
  Avallon, Yonne.
Tel: 86 34 07 86
Propr: M. Audau
Open: 15 March - 15 Nov

Twin with bath	3 D-E
Double with bath	2 E
Suites	6 G-J
(inc. breakfast)	
Total rooms:	11

No lift. 1 ground-floor room.

Table d'hôte (on
  reservation) A
  A la carte available
Chef: M. Donny Emmanuel
Lunch: 1200 - 1430
Dinner: 1830 - 2130
Specialities: *Mixte grill de*
la mer; Escargots de
Bourgogne; Salade de
langoustines fraiches; Pavé
de charolais au poivre;
Soufflé au Grand Marnier.
Demi-pension (3 days+) C-F

Groups: max. 15
Credit cards:
  Mastercard
  Visa
English & German spoken

Tennis courts
Fishing
Ballooning

13km west of the Avallon exit on Autoroute 6. From Avallon, take the D957 towards Vézelay. At Pontaubert, after 4km, turn right towards Vault-de-Lugny. The château is 500m further on the right. **Airport:** *Avallon (5km)* **Station:** *Avallon (5km)*

The original château at Vault-de-Lugny was constructed in the twelfth century, but in 1478, when Louis XI became somewhat miffed with the aristocratic owners, he ordered it to be razed to the ground - only the keep was left standing. The present building was constructed at the end of the sixteenth century - with modifications being made to the facade a century later. And a splendid place it is - a long, elegant, colour-washed building with a large central section and a russet-tiled roof.

In the mid-eighties, M. Audau began his transformation of the building and it was opened as a luxury hotel in June 1986, and everywhere is now immaculate and new-looking. A considerable amount of money and time has been lavished on every room. Several have half-panelled walls, polished wood-block floors and extremely high ceilings with huge wooden painted beams that have been decorated with intricate motifs. Some of these rooms, furnished with four-poster bed, are suites. One, the King's Bedroom, is an ideal place for indulging in macho fantasies. It has a bed large enough to accommodate at least three people and an enormous bath for two, with taps shaped like fishes and fluted matching washbasins. Other bedrooms, although more restrained, have been expensively decorated, with the fabric used to cover the walls and beds blending with the fitted carpet and the elegant upholstered chairs. All the bathrooms are extremely well equipped, usually having a double sink as well as a bath and shower. The pieces of modern reproduction furniture and the artificial flowers in many rooms jar

slightly and the saloon, with its new, traditional-styled leather chairs and its large thirties style painting of flappers was not to our taste. But there was much else that we most definitely enjoyed. The atmosphere is pleasantly relaxed and informal. The standard of service is extremely high and the courtesy and efficiency of the staff are above reproach. Best of all is the superb dining room in the vaulted cellar where guests dine at a long refectory table before a vast open fire. The food too

is excellent. Although nominally table d'hote, there is a reasonable and varied card. Outside, 800m of the River Cousin flow through the extensive and most attractive grounds with their manicured lawns and ancient trees. The cost of accommodation, especially the six suites, is not cheap, but Château de Vault-de-Lugny is an elegant yet friendly place to stay.

56 CASTEL BONAME H

☙ ★ ★
89150 Villeneuve-la-
Dondagre, Yonne.
Tel: 86 86 04 01
Proprs: H. Pierre & Mme
Helène Monthule
Open: 20 Feb - 15 Jan

Twin with shower	3 B-C
Twin with bath	7 B-C
Double with shower	2 B-C
Total rooms:	12

No lift. 4 ground-floor
rooms.

Restaurant: Open daily
Chef: M. Jean-Yves Raballand
Lunch: 1200 - 1400
Dinner: 1930 - 2130
Prix fixe: Menus at A & B
A la carte available
Specialities: *Foie gras de
Canard au Jurancon; Gigot
d'agneau; Truites Boname,
Escargots de Bourgogne;
Selon saison et marché du
jour.*
Demi-pension (3 days+)   C

Seminars: max. 10
Groups: max. 24
Receptions: max. 30
Credit cards:
    Diners Club
    Visa
English & Italian spoken
Tennis court
Swimming pool
Golf course
Sauna

La Castellerie, Relais
    du Silence

*38km south-east of Nemours and 9.5km north-east of the Courtenay exit on the A6. From
there, take the N60 (towards Sens). After 8.5km, turn left on the D370 to Villeneuve-la-
Dondagre. Turn left in the village to the château.* **Station:** *Sens (18km) or Courtenay
(10km)*

Originally built in 1860, Castel Boname is more attractive than many châteaux of
that period. The major building and its much smaller wing are finely proportioned
in a neo-classical style with large arched windows and white louvered shutters.
The decorative red brick and white stone facade is restrained. The wooded, three-
acre garden is beautifully maintained, with lawns, flower-beds, shrubs and ancient
trees.

The present owners acquired the property in 1980 and spent eight years on its
restoration. And a good job they made of it. In March 1988, it was opened as a
hotel and restaurant. The bedrooms are comfortable and the bathrooms modern
and well equipped. The saloon bar is in an ancient hunting lodge and the
restaurant is in a pretty conservatory, housing many flowers and exhibitions of
local artists' work. In summer, breakfast can be taken on the terrace or on the lawn.
In winter, special hunting parties are arranged to shoot partridges, pheasants,
woodcock, hares etc.

57 CHATEAU DE LYS PG

	Twin with bath	1 A	No credit cards
Bressolles, 03000 Moulins,	Double with bath	2 A	
Allier.	Double with shared w.c.	4 A	Fishing
Tel: 70 44 41 57	Total rooms:	7	Swimming pool 6km
Propr: M. Tavignot			
Open: All year	Table d'hôte available		Gîtes de France

7km south of Moulins. From there, take the N9. After 4.5km, pass by the village of Bressolles. After a further 2km, turn left down a road, signposted to the château, which is at the end of the road after 500m. **Airport:** *Moulins (12km)* **Station:** *Moulins (7km)*

In an incredible position, on a rise overlooking the meandering River Allier and its vast sandy banks, Château de Lys was rebuilt in the eighteenth-century on the site of a much earlier building, a tower of which still survives. Once the home of a long succession of high-ranking French army officers, the château has clearly seen better days. When M. Tavignot purchased it in the late seventies, it had fallen into a state of considerable decay. Since then, he has undertaken much of the restoration work himself, but a considerable amount still needs to be done, especially to the roof and the two towers flanking the still elegant brick and stone facade. Meanwhile, M Tavignot - a genial host - has created seven simple guests-rooms which, though clean and functional, are without the normal trappings of a château. The soft beds are comfortable and the bathrooms are simple - although a couple have lovely old and now much sought-after washbasins and bidets. There is a stone-floored, farmhouse-style kitchen and a couple of utilitarian rooms for guests. The cost of accommodation at Château de Lys is the cheapest in this guide, but it must be stressed that it's a place without frills and with only the most basic of facilities.

58 CHATEAU SAINT-JEAN H

★ ★

Parc Saint-Jean, B.P. 145,
  03100 Montlucon, Allier.
Tel: 75 05 04 65
Telex: 392 339 F
Propr: SA Saint Jean
Directors: M. James de
  Villesuzanne & M. Laurent-
  Charles Fontenit
Open: All year

Twin with bath	12 C
Double with bath	12 C
Suites (max. 4)	6 E-H
Total rooms:	30

Lift

Restaurant: Open every day
Chef: M. de Ponte
Lunch: 1230 - 1500
Dinner: 2000 - 2230
Menus at A & B
  A la carte available
Specialities: *Caviar et son
verre de vodka; Demi-homard
flambé cognac et whisky;
Oeuf dans l'oeuf au caviar;
Rognons de veau aux graines
de moutarde; Pavé de
Charolais aux deux
champignons.*
Demi-pension   D

Seminars: max. 50
Groups: max. 50
Credit cards:
  American Express
  Diners Club
  Eurocard
  Visa
English, German & Spanish
  spoken

Indoor swimming pool
Tennis court 500m
Fishing 3km
Golf course 3km

Châteaux Hôtels Indép.

In the southern suburbs of Montlucon. Leave by Avenue J. F. Kennedy (N144). Some 700m after going under the railway-bridge and at the junction where the N144 and the D1089 fork, turn right on the D604. Take the second left, which leads to the Saint-Jean Park and the château. **Station:** *Montlucon (1.5km)*

In the front of the château is a park of over ten acres which boasts of containing 487 different varieties of trees. This tranquil site once belonged to the Templars and after them to the Knights of Malta. In 1988, Château Saint-Jean, which previously had been a small eight-bedroom hotel with a popular restaurant, was substantially remodelled. The main dining room is still in the stone-vaulted twelfth-century chapel. The reputation of the restaurant continues to be high and its innovative and reasonably-priced cuisine is much praised. The major addition to the château is a large wing, built to the left of the turreted entrance. All the bedrooms and suites are now on the first and second floors of this new block. They have tiled floors, good-quality reproduction furniture and excellent beds, but, of course, they are brand-new rooms. Each bedroom has an immaculate, well-equipped bathroom. On the ground-floor of the new block is a magnificent heated swimming pool and a large area used for receptions. The beamed public rooms in the old part of the château - including the lounge and reception area - have also been refurbished with new reproduction fittings and furniture. There is very little left at Château Saint-Jean of the atmosphere of a château, but everywhere is as immaculate and as well equipped as one would expect to find in a new first-class hotel.

59 CHATEAU DE BOUSSAC PG

♡ ♡ ♡ ★ ★ ♈	Twin with bath	1 C
Target, 03140 Chantelle,	Double with bath	3 C
Allier.	Suite (max. 3)	1 D
Tel: 70 40 63 20	Total rooms:	5
Proprs: Marquis & Marquise		
de Longueil	Table d'hôte on	
Open: Open all year.	reservation (inc. wine)	B
	Dinner: 20.30	
No lift	Demi-pension (3 days+)	

Seminars: max. 10
Groups: max. 10
No credit cards
English & Spanish spoken

Swimming pool 10km

Châteaux Hôtels Indép.
Château Accueil

44km east of Montlucon and 16km south-east of the Montmarault exit on the A71. From there, cross over the N145 onto the D46 (towards Saint-Potcain-sus-Sioule). After 4.5km, after passing through Saint-Marcel-en-Murat, turn right onto the D42. 500m after crossing over the autoroute, turn right onto an unmade-up track that leads to the château. **Airport:** Vichy (50km) **Station:** *Montlucon (44km)*

This once remote château, which is now so close to an autoroute exit, is one of France's hidden historical treasures - it is also one of our favourite châteaux. Built in 1650 and totally surrounded by a moat, it has wings which enclose a quadrilateral courtyard. At the four corners of the château are tubby circular towers, topped by prim, pointed, peg-tiled roofs. The direct ancestors of the present owner purchased the estate in 1742 and have lived at Boussac ever since.

The entrance to the château is across a bridge over the moat and through the towering keep. When we arrived, we were greeted in the huge courtyard first by a couple of English collie dogs and then by the Marquis and Marquise — a charming, talented and amusing couple who contributed much to the delight and pleasure we experienced during our stay. The interior is just as impressive as the outside. Although much repair and renovation has taken place, all the rooms — including the bedrooms — are much as they would have been in the eighteenth century. There are beautiful polished wooden floors - family heirlooms and antiques are everywhere. Our bedroom was charming, decorated with a soft pink

paper and with interesting paintings on the wall. There were choice pieces of eighteenth-century furniture in the room and, in one corner, a baby grand. The bathroom was splendid. There were beautiful towels provided and cotton dressing-gowns. Through the windows, there were spectacular views across the moat and parkland.

Dinners at Boussac are a major event - sophisticated and yet not formal, friendly and extremely entertaining with most convivial company. At a long table, beautifully set, there is served an excellent selection of wine and fabulous food prepared by the Marquise, who is also responsible for the exquisite home-made butter. Breakfast is served in the bedroom.

Château de Boussac is a special and most agreeable place. Most highly recommended.

60 CHATEAU DU RIAU PG

♖ ♖ ♖	Twin bed with shower	1 C	No credit cards
03460 Villeneuve-sur-Allier,	Twin bed with bath	1 C	English, German, Italian &
Allier.	Suite	1 E	Spanish spoken
Tel: 70 43 30 74	(inc. breakfast)		
Propr: Baron & Baronne	Total rooms:	3	Swimming pool 6km
Durye			
Open: All year	No restaurant		Château Accueil
			Inter. Leading Association
No lift			

13km north of Moulins. From there, take the N7 and after the end of the dual carriageway and just before the road bends left to enter Villeneuve, turn right onto the D133. The château is on the right. **Airport:** *Vichy (65km)* **Station:** *Moulins (13km)*

Surrounded by a moat and an outer wall, this impressive château consists of a collection of fascinating buildings in various styles of Bourbon domestic and military architecture. The circular dovecote, the impressive towered gate-way and the compact main building with its two small wings were built during the fifteenth century. A row of outbuildings was added to one side of the courtyard in the seventeenth century. Outside the walls is a most unusual half-timbered tithe-barn, which was built in 1584. In its five hundred years of existence, Le Riau has been occupied by only four families. The ancestors of the present owners acquired the château in 1826.

This important historical monument is open to the public and, most afternoons, tours can be made of the interior (when the three guest-rooms are on view). All the rooms are beautifully decorated and are full of wonderful objects and interesting paintings, including work by the impressionist Emmanuel de La Villéon. A spiral stone staircase leads to the delightful bedrooms, which have high old beds and oriental rugs on the polished wooden floors. Breakfast is served either in the bedroom or in the large kitchen.

Although the château is a family home, there is a slight feel of staying in a museum. We were received politely but formally.

61 CHATEAU DE LA VIGNE PG

♥ ♥ ♥ ★ ♥
Ally, 15700 Pleaux, Cantal.
Tel: 71 69 00 20
Proprs: M. Bruno & Mme
  Anne du Fayet de la Tour
Open: 15 April - 15 Nov

No lift

Double with bath	2	B-C
Suite (max. 4)	1	C
Total rooms:	3	

No restaurant

No credit cards

Groups: max. 8
English spoken

Tennis court
Miniature golf 800m
Model car museum

Château Accueil
Inter. Leading Association

49km north of Aurillac. From there, take the D922 (towards Mauriac). After 39km, (just after the right-turn to Salers), turn left on the D680 to Ally. 5km later, turn right on the D29 to Escorailles. The château is through the village on the right. **Airport:** *Aurillac (50km)* **Station:** *Drignac/Ally (6km)*

This important historic monument is set among the mountains of high Auvergne with uninterrupted, spectacular views of the valleys below. Built in 1450, the exterior of the château is a perfect, unspoiled example of a medieval castle that would not be out of place in the Highlands of Scotland. The stone-clad buildings and towers are crowned with machicolated parapet walks.

The interior contains many treasures. The fan-vaulted and domed ceiling of the chapel is painted with simple figures of angels carrying the symbols of the Passion. The arched ceiling of the hall of justice is more intricately painted with a complex Renaissance design incorporating five portraits. All the rooms are furnished and decorated in an authentic eighteenth-century style. Hanging on the walls are elaborate tapestries and family portraits. In the main salon, there is a charming painted panel above the fireplace. The bedrooms are spectacular - light-years away from the anonymous, bland hotel bedroom. Most fantastic of all is the Chambre Troubadour, which has polished oak floorboards, carved wooden panelling, and a delightful painted ceiling. Mounted on the walls are deer antlers and standing on an ancient cupboard is an eighteenth-century ceramic crucifix. The elaborate bed is a barley-twist four-poster. Another simpler, but most appealing, bedroom has a vaulted ceiling, a stone fireplace and a country four-poster bed. We stayed

in the third bedroom which, though smaller, was delightful. It also had a four-poster bed and an open fire-place which had been thoughtfully laid — even in June the nights can be chilly in the high Auvergne. Breakfast is served in a gorgeous eighteenth-century dining room with painted wall-panels above the doors.

Bruno and Anne du Fayet de la Tour clearly have a great affection for their home and have embued it with a real feeling of warmth and welcome. They are generous and kind to guests. But theirs is primarily a family home — for themselves and their six children. The youngest of these, called Fleur, has a cherubic smile and, while we were there, an apparently insatiable passion for cheese.

Guided tours of the château are available to the public in July and August. One of the special attractions is a most unusual collection of over a thousand model cars which illustrate the history and development of motoring. But it is the château itself that is the real spectacle, embued as it is with great spirit by its owners. Most strongly recommended.

Top: **Château de Riau** (60) Allier (Auvergne)
Bottom: **Château de Roussan** (106) Bouches-du-Rhône (Provence)

Top: **Château de Boussac** (59) Allier (Auvergne)
Bottom: **Château de Codignat** (65) Puy-de-Dôme (Auvergne)

62 CHATEAU DE BASSIGNAC PG

ଓ ଓ ଓ ★ ★ ♥
Bassignac, 15240 Saignes,
   Cantal
Tel: 71 40 82 82
Proprs: M. Jean-Michel &
   Mme Annie Besson
Open: All year

No lift

Twin with bath   2 B-C
Double with bath   1 C
Suite (max. 4)   1 C
   (inc. breakfast)   4

Table d'hôte on
   reservation   B

Groups: max. 8
No credit cards
English spoken

Fishing
Tennis court 3km
Swimming pool 3km

Château Accueil

18km north-east of Mauriac. From there, take the D922 to Bassignac. The château is up a small road to the right, just before entering the village. **Airport:** *Aurillac (75km)* **Station:** *Bort-les-Orgues (14km)*

Surrounded by spectacular scenery and with its own beautiful garden, this sixteenth-century château has a pleasing, tranquil appearance that belies its origins as a fortress during the troubled times of Louis XIV. Squat and compact, the main stone-clad building has a square tower at each end of the facade and in the centre a matching square entrance section. The small-pane picture windows introduced during the eighteenth century help create the appearance of a country house. It has been in the possession of the present owner's family since 1898 and it was bought by them with all the contents from the Bassignacs, who had first built the château.

    M. and Mme Besson are a delightful couple who speak excellent English and are extremely hospitable. The evening meals are festive occasions with the very best of French home-cooking, including sausages and ham that is cured in the kitchen's vast open-fireplace. Fresh farm produce comes from their son who runs the farm and lives close-by. When the weather is warm, breakfast and dinner are taken on the splendid terrace. There is also a dining room, but we were privileged to dine in the kitchen — a delightful room, which is obviously the hub of this very friendly château.

    There is a very comfortable and welcoming atmosphere about Bassignac. The four bedrooms, with their beautiful old oak doors are some distance from each other and so are very private. All are simple — very French — with wonderful old furniture, old oak floor boards and crocheted bed-spreads. Although small, the bathrooms are charming, each having a separate w.c. Available for guests is a fascinating large, light salon with oak floor boards and oriental carpets. There is also a vast enamelled stove dating from the early nineteenth century.

Just 1.5km from the Dordogne and with a stream running through the small park, this is a calm and isolated spot, within easy reach of the main tourist centres of the upper Auvergne. Very highly recommended.

63 CHATEAU LE LAVENDES H

✠ ★ ★
Route de Neuvic, 15350
  Champagnac, Cantal.
Tel: 71 69 62 79
Proprs: M. Gérard & Mme
  Louisette Gimmig
Open: 5 March - 1 Jan

Twin with shower   6 B
Double with shower   1 B
Double with bath   1 B
    Total rooms: 8

No lift

Restaurant: Closed Tues in
  winter
Chef: M. Gérard Gimmig
Lunch: 1230 - 1330
Dinner: 1930 - 2100
Prix fixe: Menus at A & B
  A la carte available
Specialities: *Poelée de
  grenouilles aux noisettes et
  artichauts; Escalope de foie de
  canard aux radis et oignons
  confits; Saint Nectaire
  patissier.*

Demi-pension
  (min. 3 days) B

Groups: max. 10
Credit cards:
  Eurocard
  Visa
English & German spoken

Swimming pool
Sauna & solarium
Tennis court 800 m
Golf 10km

Châteaux Hôtels Indép.
Châteaux et Demeures de
  Tradition

31km north of Mauriac. From there, take the D922. After 24km, turn left onto the D15 to Champagnac. The château is a further 500 m beyond the village on the left. **Station:** *Bort-les-Orgues (13km)*

Opened as a hotel in June 1986, this stone-faced château was rebuilt in the seventeenth century on the site of a much older building, incorporating the original central stone-staircase. The strong point of this hotel is the food, and the dishes are beautifully prepared and very reasonable in price. The patisseries are splendid. Gérard Gimmig, the proprietor/chef has won many awards for them, including the Championnat de France du Dessert, awarded by La Grande Bible des Hotels et Restaurants de France. This was for his own creation, Saint Nectaire Patissier - a base of fine Genoese sponge, soaked in Kirsch and hazelcream and covered with a mousse made with soft white cheese. If you have a sweet tooth, Le Lavendès is paradise.

The château is comfortably furnished - with a few eccentric touches. The attractive dining room with its chandelier and elegant gilded mirror has vinyl floor-

---

covering. So does the salon de thé, which has a massive open fireplace. The vaulted ceiling of the fourteenth-century staircase leading to the bedrooms is painted blue and decorated with silver stars. The bedrooms are small with tiny bathrooms. A swimming pool and sauna are available for use by guests. This is a family-run hotel, and we found all its members extremely helpful and courteous. They are rightfully very proud of their enterprise.

The road that passes the château continues on, through a forest dense with oaks, beech, pine and hazel-nut, winding down a steep slope until, 2km later, it crosses the broad Dordogne River by a narrow bridge, Pont de Vernejoux. It is a beautifully tranquil spot.

64 CHATEAU DE LA BASTIDE н

	Twin with shower	4 B	Demi-pension (3 days+) B
15410 Salers, Cantal.	Twin with bath	5 B	
Tel: 71 40 70 33	Double with shower	1 B	Groups: max. 50
Propr: Mme Caby	Double with bath	3 B	Credit cards:
Open 21 Dec - 25 Oct	Total rooms:	13	Eurocard
			Visa
No lift	Restaurant (at the Hôtel des Ramparts): Open daily		

43km north of Aurillac. From there, take the N120 (towards Tulle) for 3km. Then, at the junction, turn right onto the D922. After 32km, turn right onto the D680 which leads to Salers. There is no parking at the château and the town has a jumble of narrow streets. Follow signs to Hôtel des Remparts. **Station:** *Mauriac (25km)*

Overlooking the verdant valley of the Maronne, Salers is a pretty medieval town that is one of the most popular tourist spots in the Auvergne. Château de La Bastide, which is perched above the old ramparts of the town, is used as a residential annexe by the Hôtel des Remparts — although it does have its own small, stone-floored breakfast room and bar. The château has a fifteenth-century stone exterior, but inside it has been thoroughly modernised. There are sapele doors, plastic flowers and tiled stairs. Only a few beams remain as evidence of the building's age. The bedrooms are modern - well furnished, comfortable but small, as are the bathrooms. Outside, there is a small terrace. The cost of accommodation is very reasonable. The food at the Hôtel des Remparts, which is only 100m away, is extremely good value. The proprietor and her family are very pleasant and helpful. A good tourist hotel.

☘ ★ ★ ★
Bort-l'Etang, 63190 Lezoux,
  Puy-de-Dôme.
Tel: 73 68 43 03
Telex: 990 606 F
Proprs: Mme Monique
  Barberan & M. Guy Vidal
Dir: M. Denis Lesage
Open: 24 March - 4 Nov

Twin with bath	6 C-E
Double with bath	5 E
Suites (max. 3)	3 E-F
Total rooms:	14

No lift. 1 ground-floor room.

Restaurant: Closed Tues &
  Thurs lunch (apart from
  reservations)
Chef: Freugris Beuret
Lunch: 1230 - 1315
Dinner: 1930 - 2100
Prix fixe: Menus at B
  A la carte available
Speciality: *Pot au feu de
  foie gras.*
Demi-pension (3 days+) D-E

Seminars: max. 30
Groups: max. 20
Receptions: max. 40
Credit cards:
  American Express
  Diners Club
  Eurocard
  Visa
English spoken

Swimming-pool
Horse riding 2km
Tennis court 5km
Golf course 35km

Relais & Châteaux

26km east of Clermont-Ferrand. From there, take the A720, pass over the intersection with the A71 and leave by exit one, taking the N89 to Lezoux. On the by-pass, turn right onto the D223 (towards Courpière). After 3km, turn right onto the D309 to Bort-l'Etang. Just before entering the village, turn right onto a narrow road that leads to the château. **Airport:** *Aulnat (25km)* **Station:** *Thiers (20km)*

When Château de Codignat was constructed in the fourteenth century, it was much larger than it is now. But like many ancient castles in France, it was left derelict during the nineteenth century and its stone provided the building-material for many local houses. At the beginning of this century, the part that remained was reroofed and reoccupied. It passed through various hands, including Prince Obolenski - one of several members of the Tsar's family that fled to France at the beginning of the Russian Revolution. Later, it was again left empty and desolate until, in 1971, it was acquired by Monique Barberan and transformed into an hotel.

We drove to Codignat along the D212 from Billom, passing between meadows full of wild flowers. Standing among vast chestnut trees, the beautiful château has wisteria growing up its ancient stone facade. The interior has been meticulously decorated in the traditional manner with materials covering the walls - heavy brocades, friezes and tapestries. The dining hall is in what was once the circular guard-room. A flight of lovely old stone stairs spirals up through the tower. Although not much of the furniture is antique, there are many old objects around - copper saucepans, an oil press, a suit of armour.

All the bedrooms are named after famous personalities from the fifteenth century, including Agnes Sorel, whose portrait shows her sporting the one-bare-breast fashion. Another room is named after the infamous Bluebeard. The suites and several of the bedrooms are a blaze of colour. One has purple carpet, mauve and purple walls, red, purple and blue bedspread, gold chairs, red chairs, brown ceiling and a massive, wedding-cake of a headboard, painted white with embossed gilt decorations. Another is an astonishing amalgam of leopard-skin fabric, lilac carpet, purple walls with scarlet trim and gilded headboard. There are fantasy bathrooms awash with marble and lurid murals. It's all part of the candy-floss mock-medieval world that Mme Barberan has created.

Château de Codignat has proved to be extremely popular. The facilities, including the swimming pool, are excellent, the food is superb, the welcome is warm, and the staff are extremely efficient. There is just the problem of learning to love the mauve and the purple, the gold and the green, the scarlet and the ...

66 CHATEAU LA ROCHE PG

♥ ♥ ♥ ★	Double with bath	1 B	Receptions: max. 50
Chaptuzat, 63260 Aigueperse,	Suite (max. 3)	1 C	No credit cards
Puy-de-Dôme.	Total rooms:	2	
Tel: 73 63 63 81			Tennis court 3km
Propr: Comte & Comtesse de	No lift		
Torcy	Table d'hôte on		English spoken
Open: All year	reservation B		

26km south-west of Vichy. From there, take the D984 to Aigueperse. In the town, turn left (onto the main N9) and then shortly afterwards turn right on the D12. In the village of Chaptuzat, a road to the left leads to the château. **Station:** *Vichy (26km) or Aigueperse (4km)*

La Roche is a remarkable medieval fort standing at the edge of a steep escarpment overlooking the Limagne plain. Originally built in the eleventh century and much enlarged over the following three hundred years by the Ducs de Montpensier and d'Auvergne, the feudal château was given in 1537 as a dowry to Michel de l'Hospital, who subsequently became the Chancellor of France. Originally, the castle totally enclosed a vast courtyard but, in the seventeenth century, to reveal the spectacular panorama, the side on the escarpment was demolished and replaced by a stone balustrade. Having several times passed through female descendents, La Roche, at the end of the eighteenth century, was occupied by Jean Grenier. As he supported the revolutionaries, his castle was spared. Later, Jean Grenier rallied to the cause of Louis XVIII and during the Restoration was made a baron. As an important historical monument, La Roche was first opened to the public in 1951 by the then owner, Général Baron d'Arnoux de Maison Rouge. In 1989, his daughter and her husband created two superb guest rooms in their château.

Visitors enter La Roche through an ancient gate framed by two crenellated towers. This leads into the outer courtyard and the large formal garden. Entrance to the inner courtyard is through a vaulted porch. On the ground floor of the château are many unspoiled rooms with decorated beams, fabric and stained glass

---

dating back to the sixteenth century. Vistors can view Michel de l'Hospital's bedchamber, the large seventeeth-century drawing-room, the eighteenth-century dining room and the armoury.

A spiral stone staircase leads up through the tower to the two guest rooms. In the double room, there are old oak floorboards, soft fabric on the walls and a deep red material with gold motifs on the four-poster bed. The suite is similarly furnished with pretty fabric. The splendid new bathrooms have grey and pink marble tiles. From the bedroom windows there are fantastic views. Dinner is available for guests, on reservation. A most interesting and unusual place to stay.

67 CHATEAU DE DIVONNE H

🛡🛡 ★ ★ ★
Route de Gex, 01220
  Divonne-les-Bains, Ain
Tel: 50 20 00 32
Telex: 309 033 F
Propr: M. René Traversac
  (one of his Grandes Etapes
  Françaises)
Direc: M. Guy Martin
Open: 12 March - 1 Jan

Single with bath	7 B-C
Twin with bath	6 C-E
Double with bath	10 D-E
Suites	5 E-F
Total rooms:	28

Lift. 3 ground-floor rooms.

Restaurant: Open daily, but
  closed for lunch on Tues &
  Wed in low season
Chef: M. Guy Martin
Lunch: 12.15 - 1400
Dinner: 1915 - 2130
Prix fixe: Menus at B
  A la carte available
Specialities: *Foie gras et choux*
  en raviole, sauce au jus de
  truffes: Omble chevallier
  et féra du lac; Jambonette
  de volaille de bresse
  'miéral' à l'épeautre et à
  l'orge perlé; Tarte chaude
  aux pommes, nectar de gamay
  à la maniguette; Cappuccino
  glacé.

Seminars: max. 25
Groups: max. 45
Receptions: max. 70
Credit cards:
  Visa
English, German & Italian
  spoken

Tennis court
Golf course 200m
Swimming pool 1km
Helipad

Relais & Châteaux

*19km north of Geneva. From there, take the N1 autoroute. Leave at the Divonne exit. Follow
the by-pass round and join the D984c towards Gex. The château is on the left, opposite the
golf course.* **Airport:** *Geneva (15km)* **Station:** *Geneva (15km)*

This is yet another of the luxurious château-hôtels run by the saviour of so many
important historic buildings in France — René Traversac. There has been a château
at Divonne since 1095, but that fortress was totally destroyed in 1589. The building
that replaced it was badly damaged during the French Revolution. The present
château was constructed early in the nineteenth century, when the fashionable
architectural style was neo-classical rather than the neo-Gothic extravagancies that
were soon to follow. M. Anthonioz, who was the Mayor of Divonne and an agent
of the Ministry of Tourism under General de Gaulle, was responsible for
transforming the château into a first class hotel. When he died, he left the premises
to the local authority.

In 1984, René Traversac took over the hotel and carried out a total restoration. It is now luxuriously furnished and appointed with stylish and often simple decorations - although a few of the carpets have bold, jarring patterns. There is a

spacious, tiled reception area with a grand staircase leading to a balcony above and a delightful salon with apricot walls and elegant furnishings. Upstairs, there are marbled columns in the corridor. The bedrooms and bathrooms vary in size, but all are exceptionally comfortable and furnished with beautiful antiques.

The cuisine of Guy Martin is first-class, with many new and delicious dishes, well deserving the Michelin rosette. Portions are generous and considerable use is made of regional delicacies, particularly the delicious fish found in the nearby Lake

Léman (Geneva). These include perch, pike, char, burbot and pink trout. The wine list includes an astonishing selection of Savoie wines, including many that are not

well known but well worth discovering. There are two extremely pleasant dining rooms, with cream-painted wood-panelling on the walls. In summer, guests can also dine on the terrace with its spectacular view across the parkland and Lake Léman to the Mont Blanc mountain chain — a panorama that Voltaire declared was 'the most beautiful in the world'.

68 CHATEAU D'URBILHAC H

♥ ♥ ★ ★ ★
Route de Vernoux, 07270
 Lamastre, Ardèche.
Tel: 75 06 42 11
Proprs: M. & Mme Antoine
 Xompéro
Open: 1 May - 10 Oct
Twin with shower   2 C
Twin with bath   8 C
Double with bath   3 C
 Total rooms: 13

No lift. 1 ground-floor room.

Restaurant: open every day
Chef: M. Ludovic Sinz
Lunch: 1230 - 1400
Dinner: 1930 - 2100
Prix fixe: Menus at A & B
 A la carte available
Specialities: *Gelée de
 lapereau à la crème de
 ciboulette; Filet de
 daurade grillé à la
 tapenade et sa marinade
 croquante de légumes; Pièce
 d'agneau rôtie, ragoût
 d'abats et pâtes fraîches à
 la farine de châtaignes.*

Demi-pension (obligatory
 in July & Aug) C

Seminars: max. 25
Groups: max. 25
Credit cards:
 American Express
 Diners Club
 Visa
English & Italian spoken

Swimming pool
Tennis court
Fishing

*42km west of Valence. From there, take the winding D533 to Lamastre, where turn left onto
the D2 towards Vernoux. The château is a further 2km.* **Airport:** *Valence (48km)* **Station:**
Valence (42km)

It's a long, twisting road that leads to this isolated and peaceful spot high above
the small town of Lamastre. The Renaissance-style château was built for a local
lawyer at the end of the last century on the foundations of a sixteenth-century
fortification. Sturdy and solid, it makes no pretence to be older than it is and the
interior remains a perfect evocation of the period in which it was built. There is
much heavy wooden panelling (even around the arched opening from the entrance
hall); some ceilings are beamed, others have wooden coving; in the salon there is
a highly polished parquet floor. The furniture, paintings and even many of the
curtains are also of the period — which tends to make some of the rooms seem
sombre and dark. The bedrooms are incredibly varied, but all have tremendous
character and splendid pieces of antique furniture. Most rooms have traditional
French heavy box-beds, some covered with exotic fur covers and others with
beautiful white crochet-work - all are very pleasant and extremely comfortable. On
the second floor, the bedrooms are smaller and cheaper.

In 1989, a new dining room was opened in a large glass pavilion at the rear of the château. It is an extremely pleasant place, with a pretty alpine garden immediately outside. Guests, while they dine, can watch the chef and his assistants at work in the new glass-fronted kitchen close-by. The food is very good indeed. This is not the kind of place which tourists are likely to stumble across by accident. It is used by people wanting to spend a few days exploring or relaxing in a remote mountain area, while staying at a hotel with good food and other amenities. And it is a splendid spot. From the walled terrace, with its flower-baskets and statues of demure ladies, there is a delightful view across the swimming pool of the dense woods and lush farm-land stretching down into the valley below. Highly recommended.

69 CHATEAU LE SCIPIONNET H

♥ ♥ ★ ★
07140 Les Vans, Ardèche.
Tel: 75 37 23 84
Propr: M. Jean Dupouy
Open: 15 March - 1 Nov

Twin with shower	4 C
Twin with bath	10 C
Double with shower	2 C
Double with bath	8 C
Suites (max. 5)	3 D
Total rooms:	27

Lift

Restaurant: Open every day
Chef: M. Hocéne Boufeoja
Lunch: 1230 - 1400
Dinner: 2000 - 2130
Prix fixe: Menus at B
A la carte available
Specialities: *Terrine de
grenouille à la menthe;
Foie gras de canard frais;
Matelote d'anguille;
Fromages du pays.*
Demi-pension (2 days+) B-C

Seminars: max. 45
Groups: max. 25
Credit cards:
American Express
Diners Card
Visa
English, German & Italian
spoken

Swimming pool
Tennis courts

Châteaux Hôtels Indép.
Relais du Silence

*46km north of Alès. From there, take the D904 (which later becomes the D104) through
Saint-Ambroix. 2km after Saint-Paul-le-Jeune, turn left on the D901 to Les Vans. There,
turn right on the D104a. 2km later, turn left onto a narrow road, signposted to the château.
It is a further 1km.* **Airport:** *Nimes (95km)* **Station:** *Villefort (28km)*

Replacing a much older building, this château was constructed in 1875 amidst a
plantation of mulberry trees beside a fast-flowing river. Designed in the romantic
style, the white faced building with its gentle-sloping tiled roof has three small
towers topped with thin turrets. The small, pleasant reception area opens onto a
large, bright open-space with a central stair-well. Plants thrive in the sunlight that
streams through the windows and the white walls are ablaze with modern works
of art. There are several pleasant public rooms, including a lounge crammed with
period furniture and various 'conversation-pieces', and a small library. The two
light and airy dining rooms are charming, with windows that open onto the garden
and surrounding woodland. The bedrooms differ considerably in decoration and
size - but all, though modest, are comfortable.
    Situated in a remote area between the gorges of the Tarn and the Ardèche,
Château le Scipionnet is surrounded by its own 25-acre estate. Catering mainly for

those staying at least a few days, the hotel provides several activities for its guests. There are tennis courts, a swimming pool and a pleasant terrace. In the grounds are what appear to be the remains of an ancient viaduct. In fact, it is a decorative wall, built to restrain the hill-side behind.

There is at Le Scipionnet a most relaxed and pleasant atmosphere. We found M. and Mme Dupouy to be a charming, helpful couple. Interested in the arts, they arrange at the château many exhibitions of paintings and antiques, as well as occasional musical and literary soirées. It is not the place to indulge in a posh weekend, but it's an ideal place either to spend a relaxing holiday or to use as a base while exploring the area. Strongly recommended.

70 HOSTELLERIE DU CHATEAU DE SAMPZON H

Route d'Alès, Sampzon,
  07120 Ruoms, Ardèche.
Tel: 75 39 67 14
Direc: M. Michel Rius
Open: 1 March - 15 Oct

No lift

Twin with shower	2 B	Credit cards:
Twin with bath	9 B	American Express
Double with bath	1 B	Diners Club
Total rooms:	12	Visa

Restaurant: Open daily   Italian & Spanish spoken
Prix fixe: Menus at A
A la carte available

47km north-east of Alès. From there, take the D904 (towards Aubenas). After 19km, at Saint-Ambroxi, the road (still going towards Aubenas) becomes the D104. After a further 20km, leave the D104, which turns left, and carry on the D111 (towards Ruoms). 9km later, and just after crossing the railway line for the second time, turn right onto the small track that leads after 200m to the château. **Station:** *Aubenas (28km)*

Who could ignore a vast sixteenth-century castle with a large knife and fork sign stuck atop its once elegant main tower? Not us. We were, however, disappointed to discover that, although its substantial walls are all intact, the fascinating Château de Sampzon is empty, deserted and slowly crumbling away. The hostellerie is in the grounds — a plain, modern stone-building. We would have turned round and been on our way, but we'd had an extremely long drive on a very hot day and we were thirsty, hungry and tired. So we ventured in. The upside-down wallpaper in the reception area lent an air of eccentricity to what was otherwise a simple, modern hotel. The rooms are all clean and comfortable. The restaurant is not unpleasant, the food adequate and the service brisk. The director/chef, M. Rius, is extremely affable and helpful. Without any pretensions, it is a reasonably cheap place to stay in the shadow of a romantic castle that only a country with such a superfluity of them as France would allow to decay.

71 CHATEAU DE CLAVEL H

♥ ♥ ★ ★

Quartier des Pecolets, 26800
  Etoile-sur-Rhône, Drôme.
Tel: 75 60 61 93
Propr: M. Xavier Wemert
Open: 15 March - 1 Jan

Twin with bath   13 B-C
Double with bath   10 B-C
Suites (max. 4)   4 C-D
  Total rooms: 27

No lift

Restaurant: Open daily
Chef: M. Henri Quirici
Lunch: 1200 - 1330
Dinner: 2000 - 2230
Prix fixe: Menus at A & B
  A la carte available
Specialities: *Assiette
  Neptune aux trois poissons
  et trois sauces; Truffe
  noire du tricastin en
  escarelle; Mignon de veau
  à la crême de foie gras
  truffé.*
Demi-pension (3 days+) B-C

Seminars: max. 30
Groups: max. 50
Credit cards:
  American Express
  Eurocard
  Visa
English & German spoken

Swimming pool
Tennis court
Horse riding

Châteaux Hôtels Indép.
Inter. Leading Association

12km south of Valence (and exit from Autoroute 7). Take the D7. After 10km, it becomes the N7. Shortly afterwards, at the village La Paillasse, turn left. At the next junction, turn right towards Les Pecolets. The road to the château is a little further on the left, close to a large grain silo. **Airport:** *Valence (18km)* **Station:** *Valence (12km)*

We didn't get off to a very good start at this château. Having made a booking and telephoned to confirm it, we arrived on a Saturday to find a wedding celebration in full swing and no trace of our reservation. The reception staff appeared not at all perturbed. Eventually, but only after our normal good-temper had evaporated, a room was found for us — at a motel some 10km away. Philosophically, we returned the following day and found the staff to be in as much chaos as the previous evening. How things seem to have changed from a couple of years before that visit. Then, the owner, M. Wemert, was ever-present and described his hotel to us as having 'no events, no special activities — just a smooth way of life!'

Clavel is an imposing, white-stone château, set amidst open countryside in a 15-acre estate, that includes woods, meadows, a lake and an area for riding horses. Built as a family home in 1870, the front of the château has many stone balconies overlooking the large terrace and the pretty garden. At the back is the swimming pool and tennis court. Inside, there is a large central hall with a gigantic chandelier and at the very top of the building a vast stained-glass skylight. The public telephone is in an old sedan-chair. Much of the furniture in the public rooms is either modern or reproduction, but there are a few nice antiques. The dark-green dining room is pleasant and the food good. Across the courtyard at the rear of the château, there is a vast arched room used for banquets and receptions. The bedrooms are comfortable and a couple have four-poster beds. The decorations are usually inoffensive, although there is very florid wallpaper in some of the bedrooms. We welcome reports.

72 CHATEAU DE MONTBOUCHER

Restaurant Le Castel H

★ ★
BP5, 26740 Montboucher-sur-
  Jabron, Drôme.
Tel: 75 46 08 16
Telex: 306 022 F
Fax: 75 01 44 09
Propr: M. Bernard Loiseau
Open: 1 Dec - 1 Oct

No lift

Twin with bath	4	B-C
Double with bath	6	B-C
Suite (max. 4)	1	C
Total rooms:	11	

Restaurant: Open daily
Chef: M. Stefan Borowski
Lunch: 1200 - 1400
Dinner: 1930 - 2100
Prix fixe: Menus at A
  A la carte available
Demi-pension (3 days+) B-C

Groups: max. 20
Credit cards:
  American Express
  Diners Club
  Visa
English spoken

Swimming pool
Tennis court 500m
Practice golf course 500m

La Castellerie

Close to the A7 and 4.5km east of Montélimar. From there, take the D940. After 4km, and just before the road passes underneath the A7, turn left to the village of Montboucher-sur-Jabron. At a T-junction in the village, turn left and then right. The château is on the right.
Airport: *Orange (58km)* **Station:** *Montélimar (5km)*

From the thirteenth century, a castle has stood on this hill-site, overlooking the Rhône Valley. The present château was constructed early in the nineteenth century. It was bought in 1970 by the present owner, who converted it into a delightfully French, small hotel. It has little feeling of an historic château, but the bedrooms are charming, the lounge — with its unusual reflective ceiling — is comfortable, and served in the dining room are good traditional dishes at a most reasonable price. Outside, there is a swimming pool and fine terrace with spectacular views.

73 CHATEAU DE ROCHEGUDE H

♕ ♕ ★ ★
26790 Rochegude, Drôme.
Tel: 75 04 81 88
Telex: 345 661 F
Proprs: Union of Wine
 Growers
Director: M. André Chabert
Open: 1 March - 31 Dec

Single with bath	2 C
Twin ·with bath	11 D-F
Double with bath	12 D-F
Suites (max. 4)	4 I-K
Total rooms:	29

Lift. 3 ground-floor rooms.

Restaurant: Closed mid-day
 on Tues & Wed in low
 season
Chef: M. Eric Coisel
Lunch: 1230 - 1400
Dinner: 1930 - 2100
Prix fixe: Menu at B
 A la carte available
Specialities: *Ravioles de
 Romans au consommé de
 canette et truffe; Noisette
 et rognons d'agneau en
 créinette au thym et
 romarin; Soufflé léger aux
 pistaches et noix de coco.*

Seminars: max. 50
Groups: max. 40
Credit cards:
 American Express
 Diners Club
 Visa
English, German, Italian &
 Spanish spoken

Swimming pool
Tennis court
Horse riding 8km

Relais & Chateaux

14km north of Orange. From there, take the N7. After 3km, turn right onto the D976, but then take the first left onto the D117 to Rochegude. **Airport:** *Nimes (65km)* **Station:** *Orange (14km)*

Château de Rochegude stands on a rocky bluff overlooking the plain of the Rhône valley, north of Orange. There has been a fortress there since at least the third century, when it offered protection to pilgrims and travellers on the famous Via Agrippa. Over the centuries that followed, it was frequently attacked and repaired, partially destroyed and then rebuilt. A twelfth-century keep still survives, but most of the existing building was constructed during the reign of Louis XIV, towards the end of the seventeenth century. Later, decorative stone work was added to the facade, mellowing the otherwise rather austere appearance.

Now the château is a most distinguished hotel, furnished with many antiques. Most of the bedrooms are spacious. There are many fine touches throughout the château, including the arched (and now glass-enclosed) loggia with its stone sculptures. The dining room is a fittingly elegant place for the excellent cuisine that

is rightly famed — a Michelin rosette, among other recognition — for its classical dishes, prepared with great flair. From the terrace, there is a splendid view over the extensive grounds to the vineyards of the Rhône.

At the beginning of 1989, after long being the property of the Galibert family, Rochegude changed ownership. It has been purchased by the local union of wine growers. Perhaps this will mean that new investment will be made in the hotel — and it is necessary. Despite its grand reputation, we found (in June 1989) that the château had the air of being well worn, though well loved — rather like a comfortable shoe. Many small things needed changing. In our bathroom — as in several others we saw — there were tacky gilt fixtures, a plastic toilet seat with a Paisley design and rather aging wallpaper. On our bed there were pink sheets that clashed violently with the orange blankets. It must be said, however, that we spoke to a number of guests who were overjoyed with their rooms and the whole atmosphere of the château. Certainly, the staff is excellent and the standard of service is above reproach.

74 CHATEAU DE COUDREE H

♥ ♥ ★ ★

Sciez, 74140 Douvaine,
  Haute-Savoie.
Tel: 50 72 62 33
Telex: 309 047 F
Propr: the Laden family
Director: M. Pierre Laden
Open: 25 April - 31 Oct

No lift. 3 ground-floor
  chalets in the park

Twin with bath	10 D-H	
Double with bath	10 D-H	
Total rooms:	20	

Restaurant: Open every day
Lunch: 1230 - 1400
Dinner: 1930 - 2130
Prix fixe: Menus at B
  A la carte available
Demi-pension (3 days+) D-F

Groups: max. 35
Credit cards:
  American Express
  Diners Club
  Visa
English & German spoken

Swimming pool
Tennis court

Relais & Châteaux

24km north-east of Geneva. From there, take the N5 through Douvaine. 7.5km later (and 1km after the left turn to Sciez), turn left onto the narrow road that leads to the château. **Airport:** *Geneva (28km)* **Station:** *Thonon-les-Bains (8km)*

Château de Coudrée was constructed mainly in the eighteenth century, but between 1911 and 1914 it was totally renovated, both inside and out. The owner, M. Bartholoni, determined to give back to the interior the grandeur that it had once possessed. He employed the Leonardi brothers — Italian antique dealers based in Paris — to find the necessary materials. They did so with gusto. The panelling for the Renaissance salon came from Florence, as did the fragment of an ancient fresco mounted above the fire-place. The panelling in the hotel bar was also brought from Italy. In the chapel, the painted ceiling is a copy of that in the chapel of the Swiss guards in the Vatican. The chimney and the parquet floor in the library were made in the style of Louis XIV, while the panelling (like that in the grand salon on the first floor) was made during the reign of Louis XV and came from an old hotel in Saint-Ouen. Fine tapestries were made from original drawings by Reubens. And so it went on. On its own, every item is impressive; but together they present a visually discomforting confusion of styles. The hotel is in some ways similar. It provides everything — sauna, bar, discotheque, private beach on the lake, windsurfing, wharf, restaurants and catering for vast receptions. It is always busy and so, just because of that, it will not suit everyone.

---

75 CHATEAU DE LA COMMANDERIE H

♥ ★
17 Avenue d'Echirolles, 38320
  Eybens, Isère.
Tel: 76 25 34 58
Proprs: M. & Mme Henri de
  Beaumont
Open: All year

No lift. 4 ground-floor
  rooms.

Twin with shower	3 B
Twin with bath	23 B
Double with bath	3 B
Total rooms:	29

No restaurant - room service
  available

Seminars: max. 25
Groups: max. 12

Credit cards:
  American Express
  Diners Club
  Visa
English & Spanish spoken

Swimming pool
Tennis court 500m
Horse riding 2km
Golf course 4km

Châteaux Hôtels Indép.

5km south-east of the centre of Grenoble. From there, take the D5 (Avenue Jean Perrot) to Eybens. After the fly-over, take the first right (there is an Esso garage on the corner) and then first left. The château is on the left. **Airport:** *Grenoble (12km)* **Station:** *Grenoble (5km)*

This plain grey stucco building is an interesting mixture of shapes and sizes. Two small towers flank the back, while another large one dominates the front. The present château was largely built in the seventeenth century, but the site is an ancient one that belonged first to the Templars and then to the Knights of Malta. After the Revolution, it became the property of Casinur Perrier, a minister of state during the reign of Charles X and an ancestor of the present owner, who converted the château into an hotel.

Some of the interior design and furniture is most attractive, with interesting antique pieces and tapestries. Other things clash, like the bright red plastic chairs in the vast eighteenth-century salon. The bedrooms are a reasonable size and comfortable, with old-style furniture and modern amenities, such as a television and telephone. Outside, the grounds are full of mature trees and bushes. Chairs and tables are grouped around the lawns. This is a reasonably-priced hotel that is only a few minutes away from the centre of Grenoble.

76 LE CHATEAU H

⚑ ⚑ ★ ★ ★ ♥
38110 Faverges-de-la-Tour,
  Isère
Tel: 74 97 42 52
Telex: 300 372 F
Proprs: M. Jo & Mme
  Catherine Tournier
Open: 1 May - 30 Sep

Twin with bath	24 E-H
Double with bath	16 E-H
Suites (max. 3)	3 J
Total rooms:	43

(The cheaper rooms are in
an annexe)

Lift. 3 ground-floor rooms.

Restaurant: Closed Mon,
  except July & Aug
Chef: M. Christian
  Gommariello
Lunch: 1230 - 1400
Dinner: 1945 - 2145
Prix fixe: Menus at B & C
  A la carte available
Specialities: *Feuilleté de
  Saint Jacques et grenouilles
  des dombes aux jeunes
  l'oiseaux; poussin du peys aux
  nouilles fraiches.*
Demi-pension (3 days+) H-L

Seminars: max. 40
Groups: max. 40
Credit cards:
  American Express
  Diners Club
  Visa
English, German & Italian
  spoken

Swimming pool
Tennis courts
Practice golf
Gymnastic room
Sauna

Relais & Châteaux

9km north-east of La-Tour-du-Pin and its exit on the A43. Take the N516 (towards Aix-les-Bains) and, after 7km at la Bâtie-Montgascon, turn left onto the D145c to Faverges-de-la-Tour. **Airport:** *Lyon (42km)* **Station:** *La Tour-du-Pin (9km)*

This elegant, square château of the Second Empire has a tower protruding from its side like a spare thumb. It's all that's left of an ancient castle that was built in the thirteenth century in what was then a strategic position.

After standing empty for twenty years, the property was bought in 1980 by Jo and Catherine Tournier, well-known local hoteliers, who have since spent a fortune on transforming it into a luxury hotel. The furnishings and decoration have been selected with great aplomb and those who like lavish surroundings will thoroughly enjoy a stay here. The grand Italian-style entrance hall has a marble mosaic floor, marble pillars and columns, a magnificent double staircase with an intricate wrought-iron balustrade, black statues, and giant ornamental urns. Walking into the hotel is somewhat like stepping onto the set of a spectacular

Hollywood musical being made in the fifties. The dining room on the lower ground floor is very attractive. There are white rough-cast walls, pink tablecloths covered with white lace, and black-framed, richly-patterned tapestry-upholstered chairs. The cuisine has won high fame. The bedrooms vary in size, but in each room there is matching fabric, often at windows, on chairs, cushions, headboards, lampshades and anything else that stood still long enough. The walls are plain, bold colours. The furniture is an agreeable mix of antiques and good-quality reproduction. No two rooms are the same, but no detail has been overlooked in any of them. The twenty cheaper rooms are in a converted farm-building and are rather like pretty rustic cottages, with their own terrace. The facilities provided are impressive. There's an outdoor terrace for dining during the summer, a vast swimming pool, two tennis courts, a sauna and a small gymnasium. The gardens have been beautifully landscaped. The staff is very efficient and friendly.

A splendid and stylish, if somewhat expensive, place to stay. Highly recommended.

77 CHATEAU DE BOIS FRANC PG

♥ ♥ ★
Jarnioux, 69640 Denice,
Rhône.
Tel: 74 68 20 91
Proprs: M. & Mme Robert
  Doat
Open: All year

No lift

Suites (max. 4)   2 C-D
(When suite not booked, a
  double room with bath is
  available   B)

No restaurant

No credit cards

English & German spoken

Horse-riding 6km
Wine-tasting

Les Etapes François Coeur

8km west of Villefranche-sur-Saône (and its exit on Autoroute 6). Leave the town by the D38 towards Roanne. 300m after the Elf garage, turn right onto the D31 through the village of Chervinges. The château is a further 4km on the left. **Airport:** *Lyon (37km)* **Station:** *Villefranche (8km)*

Built in 1860 in the style of Napoleon III, this pleasant château of mellowed white stone has a central semi-hexagonal tower. The large shuttered windows are crowned with carved stone pediments. The neat slated roof is pierced with several tall brick chimneys. The château is at the centre of a famous Beaujolais vineyard. Both are owned by M. Doat, who with his son, Thierry, is responsible for the excellent wine that is made and bottled at the château. The vast, arched wine-cave close to the château is widely accepted as being one of the most elegant in the region. Vines grow all around, and from the château's terrace, there are splendid, uninterrupted views of the Beaujolais region.

The two comfortably-furnished suites are on the first floor — one is at the front of the house and the other at the back. Both consist of three rooms (one with a double bed and the other two with single beds). Within the self-contained unit, there is a bathroom, a separate w.c. and several wash-basins. If the whole suite is not booked, it is possible to rent the double room separately. Clearly, reservations at Bois Franc are essential. Staying at Château de Bois Franc is an opportunity to experience and observe the life of a flourishing vineyard. Recommended.

---

78 CHATEAU DE PIZAY H

🛡 ★ ★

Saint-Jean-d'Ardières, 69220
  Belleville-sur-Saône, Rhône.
Tel: 74 66 51 41
Telex: 305 772 F
Propr: Mutualités Agricoles
  du Sud-Est
Direc: M. Daniel Lobjoie
Open: All year

Twin with bath   16 C
Double with bath   32 C
Suites (max. 4)   2 C-D
  Total rooms: 50
All rooms on ground floor

Restaurant: Open daily
Lunch: 1230 - 1430
Dinner: 1930 - 2130
Prix fixe: Menus at A & B
  A la carte available
Specialities: *Les trois*
  feuillantines du donjon;
  Filet de boeuf clouté;
  Pigeon aux trois épices;
  Loup en beurre d'orange;
  Salade légère au foie gras.
Demi-pension (2 days+) D

Seminars: max. 60
Groups: max. 30
Receptions: max. 30
Credit cards:
  American Express
  Diners Club
  Eurocard
  Visa
English, German & Italian
  spoken
Swimming pool
Tennis court

Relais du Silence
Hostellerie du Vignoble

7km from the Belleville exit on Autoroute 6. 26km south of Mâcon. From there, take the N6. After 20 km, at Saint-Jean-d'Ardières, turn right onto the D69 through Pizay. The château is a further 1km on the right. **Airport:** *Lyon (55km)* **Station:** *Mâcon (26km)*

The Beaujolais wines of Château de Pizay have been famous since the Middle Ages. The precious vines grow all around the château, part of which dates from the fourteenth century. Inside there are some beautiful rooms, especially the Salle du Cuvage, with its exquisite painted ceiling. The château itself is now used exclusively for receptions, seminars and dining. All the accommodation is in new chalets built around the swimming pool and tennis court. Each of the suites contains a sitting-room, bathroom and bedroom. They are attractive, if slightly anonymous, and are equipped with telephone, television and video. The cuisine is splendid and naturally the wine-list includes the château's excellent Beaujolais and Morgon. The hotel is a pleasing place to stay with very comfortable, modern accommodation.

79 CHATEAU DE CHERVINGES H

♛ ★ ★

69400 Villefranche-sur-Saône, Rhône.
Tel: 74 65 29 76
Telex: 380 772 F
Propr: The Legros Family
Director: Mme Legros & Sons
Open: 1 March - 15 Dec

Twin with shower	3 C-D
Twin with bath	3 D
Double with shower	1 D
Double with bath	3 D-E
Suites	4 F-G
Total rooms:	14

Lift

Restaurant: Closed Sun eve & Mon, except high season.
Chef: M. Olivier Legros
Lunch: 1200 - 1330
Dinner: 1930 - 2100
Prix fixe: Menus at B
A la carte only
Specialities: *Les trois amusettes du château (foie gras, crawfish & artichoke hearts with morels); Tourte aux truffes; Mosaique de légumes; Foie gras pommes au calvados.*
Demi-pension (3 days+) D

Seminars: max. 30
Groups: max. 20
Credit cards:
  American Express
  Diners Club
  Visa
English, German & Spanish spoken

Swimming pool
Tennis court
Horse riding 5km
Golf course 15km

Châteaux Hôtels Indép.

2km east of Villefranche-sur-Saône (and 5km from its exit on Autoroute 6). From the centre of the town, take the D38 towards Roanne. The château is on this road in the village of Chervinges. **Airport:** *Lyon (35km)* **Station:** *Villefranche (4km)*

Built in 1705 on the site of an eleventh-century monastery, Chervinges is an elegant three-storeyed château with cream-painted, rendered walls and white louvered shutters at the many windows. During the eighteenth century, it was the home of nobility, but that came to an end during the French Revolution when, in 1793, a mob arrived and assassinated the owner, Comte de Gravillon, the chief magistrate of Lyon. For a time, Madame Rolland, the celebrated revolutionary, lived at the château and during the nineteenth century it was the home of silk-workers. Now it is an expensive hotel used by tourists visiting this important wine-growing area. *Tempora mutantur.*

    The château is immaculately furnished and decorated, the bedrooms overlooking the pretty park are enormous and the cuisine is first-class. Beaujolais from the château's vineyard is also on sale. A smart, expensive place to stay.

LE BOURGET-DU-LAC RHONE-ALPES - Savoie

80 CHATEAU-HOTEL 'L'OREE DU LAC' H

★★	Twin with bath 5 C-D	Credit cards:
La Croix Verte, 73370 Le Bourget-du-Lac, Savoie.	Double with bath 4 D	American Express
Tel: 79 25 24 19	Suites (max. 4) 3 F	Diners Club, Visa
Telex: 309 773 F	Total rooms: 12	English, German & Italian spoken
Propr: Mme Jean-Pierre Prud'homme	Table d'hôte (on reservation) A	Swimming pool
Open: 1 Feb - 15 Dec		Tennis court
		Golf course 10km
	Seminars: max. 25	
No lift. 1 ground-floor room.	Groups: max. 10	Châteaux Hôtels Indép.

Close to Autoroute 41 and 11km south-west of Aix-les-Bains. From there, take the N201. After 7km, turn right onto the N211, beside the lake, to Le Bourget-du-Lac. **Airport:** *Chambéry/Aix (3km)* **Station:** *Aix-les-Bains (11km)*

This tall white château is in a delightful position, only 100m from Lake Bourget and in grounds of over four acres that include a splendid swimming pool and tennis court. Inside, there is the atmosphere of a cultivated home rather than of an hotel. The owners, M. and Mme Prud'homme, are architects and designers. They like their home to create a sense of well-being in their guests. Many of the walls are decorated with fine modern art, antique mirrors, and objets d'art — all creating an interesting environment. In the sitting-room, a bureau-bookcase stands next to squashy leather settees and an ancient harp. Oriental rugs cover the polished wooden floors. The bedrooms are excellent. The walls are plain soft colours, harmonising with the delicate pastel shades of the fabrics. Each room has a table and chairs, so that breakfast can be taken privately if desired. Table d'hôte can be provided, on reservation, in the attractive stone-walled dining room. There is also a private entrance from the château to M. Jean Jacob's famed restaurant, Le Bateau Ivre (two Michelin rosettes). L'Orée du Lac is a delightful château-hôtel. Recommended.

81 CHATEAU DE COLLONGES H

♥ ♥ ★ ★
Ruffieux, 73310 Chindrieux, Savoie.
Tel: 79 54 27 38
Proprs: M. & Mme Jean-Paul Gérin
Open: 6 Feb - 6 Jan

Twin with bath	4 C-D
Double with bath	5 C-D
Total rooms:	9

No lift

Restaurant: Closed Mon & Tues lunch, except high season
Lunch: 1230 - 1345
Dinner: 1930 - 2130
Prix fixe: Menus at A & B
A la carte available
Specialities: *Panaché de foie gras; Salade gourmande; Ris de veau braisé au coulis de homard.*
Demi-pension (3 days+)   C

Groups: max. 15
Credit cards:
  American Express
  Diners Club
  Visa
English spoken

Swimming pool
Tennis court 250m
Horse riding 5km

Châteaux Hôtels Indép.
Inter. Leading Association

21km north of Aix-les-Bains. From there, take the D991, along the eastern side of Lac du Bourget. After 20km, turn right into the village of Ruffieux. **Airport:** *Chambéry/Aix (30km)* **Station:** *Aix-les-Bains (21km)*

Standing high above what is said to be the largest poplar plantation in Europe, this pretty little château is a mixture of periods and styles. Building began in the fourteenth century - the tower and arched entrance to the courtyard date from that period. The rest of the building was added within the next two hundred years. The surrounding gardens are exquisite and the view from the terrace is spectacular. Nor does the interior disappoint. Stone stairs lead from the main hall with its supporting classical columns to the charming bedrooms above. Great efforts have been made to create an appropriate atmosphere — there is period furniture throughout and above the beds are elaborate drapes. The public rooms include a library with antiques and rare books. Some of the ceilings are beautifully painted, while in the dining room the walls are bare stone and a log fire blazes in the hearth. The food is good and with a sensible choice of menus. M. and Mme Gérin have achieved a tremendous amount since they acquired the ancient château and first opened it as a hotel in 1984. They are charming and informal hosts. An excellent place.

Top: **Château Le Scipionnet** (69) Ardèche (Rhone-Alpes)
Bottom: **Le Château** (76) Isère (Rhone-Alpes)

Top: **Domaine Saint Martin** (102) Alpes-Maritime (Provence)
Bottom: **Château des Alpilles** (105) Bouches-du-Rhône (Provence)

82 DOMAINE D'ESTARAC PG

★

Bages, 11100 Narbonne,
  Aude.
Tel: 68 41 57 31
Propr: M. Alexandre Van der
  Elst
Open: All year

No lift

Double with shower	3 A	
Double - shared w.c.	2 A	
(inc. breakfast)		
Total rooms:	5	
(3 rooms have extra bed)		
Apartment	1	

No restaurant

Groups: max. 12
No credit cards
English & Dutch spoken

Salt lake 4km
Tennis court 5km
Sea 7km

Gîites de France

Close to Autoroute 9, and 8km south of Narbonne. From there, take the N9 and at the end of the small village of Prat-de-Cest turn left on to a small track that goes under the A9 and continues to the château. **Airport:** *Perpignan (51km)* **Station:** *Narbonne (8km)*

A pot-holed road wends through vineyards and olive-groves to Domaine d'Estarac, a tall white-washed building in the Catalan style. It was built at the beginning of the nineteenth century for a general in Napoleon's army. A steep flight of steps leads to the tiny entrance hall. There is no sitting-room or dining room for guests. The bedrooms are basic, but comfortable. When we visited, our room was the only one at the side of the house and, one very warm night, it was difficult to sleep with the windows open, because of the constant, distant drone of traffic on the autoroute. Breakfast is served either in the bedroom or in a delightful rear-courtyard, shaded by an old mulberry tree. Unfortunately, to reach it, guests have to walk out of the front door and round to the back of the building. The young Dutch owners are kind and helpful. Their home is not really a château, but it is an exceptionally cheap place to stay, close to a part of the coast that is far less visited than most. Yet it is a beautiful, wild region, where the air is full of the unceasing whirr of crickets and the heady perfume of wild thyme and pine trees.

---

83 CHATEAU DE LA BARTHE н

★

Belflou, 11419 Salles-sur-
l'Hers, Aude.
Tel: 68 60 32 49
Propr: M. Urbain Cazanave
Open: All year

Double - shared w.c.   5 A
(inc. breakfast)
2 rooms have extra bed
No lift

Restaurant: Open daily
Lunch: 1230 - 1430
Dinner: 1930 - 2100
Prix fixe: 4 menus at A
A la carte available
Demi -pension (7 days+)   A
Specialities: *Cassoulet au
confit; Foie gras maison;
Magret grillé.*

Groups: max. 10
No credit cards
English, German &
Spanish spoken

Beside lake
Tennis courts 5km
Horse riding 7km

Gîtes de France

25km west of Castelnaudary (and exit on Autoroute 61). From there, take the D624. After 18km, at the junction with the D625, turn right to Salles-sur-l'Hers. There, turn right. At the next junction, turn right and then almost immediately left on the D333. 6km further, the road that leads to the château is on the right. **Station:** *Castelnaudary (25km)*

La Barthe is surrounded by miles of rolling hills through which wend tiny lanes with hedgerows full of wild flowers and butterflies. The long driveway down to the château is lined with wind-bent pines and ancient cypress trees. When we arrived, we searched in vain for anything resembling a château. Having driven around the adjacent caravan site, we were forced to accept that the squat, ugly stone building we'd first seen was La Barthe. It is in fact a very old priory, dating back to 1664, but there is little evidence of this, apart from an ornate gateway into the rear courtyard. Inside has been totally renewed recently in a simple, country style. The walls are rough plastered and white-washed; the ceilings and floors are pine. The dining room is large, with a stone fireplace and pine tables covered with white cloths. Bright red napkins add a splash of colour. Through the back door is the lovely, grassy courtyard, which is shaded by an old sycamore tree propped up with a Cathar cross from the Middle Ages. As we sat out there, eating a delicious and improbably cheap meal, shafts of gentle evening sunlight shone on the bare stone of the ancient walls, while doves cooed in the eves — it was a singularly tranquil experience.

The bedrooms upstairs are small and recently renovated in the simplest of styles. The mattresses are protected with plastic sheeting — which makes it seem as if you're sleeping in a home for the incontinent. The communal shower and w.c. are at one end of a long corridor.

The owner, Urbain Cazanave, his wife and daughters are delightful. Up to a few years ago, they were a farming family, living in a remote rural area. Then, in 1980, a vast reservoir was constructed in the valley at the bottom of their land. Suddenly, the drive to their farmhouse became a major access road to a place where people can swim, fish, sail and wind-surf. At present, it is known and visited by only a few. That inevitably will change. But for the moment we can report that, of all the châteaux in this book, La Barthe is almost the cheapest but by no means the least enjoyable place to stay.

84 DOMAINE D'AURIAC H

★★★
Route Saint-Hilaire, 11000
  Carcassonne, Aude.
Tel: 60 25 72 22
Telex: 500 385 F
Fax: 68 47 35 54
Proprs: M. Bernard & Mme
  Anne-Marie Rigaudis
Open: 1 Feb - January

Double with bath	21 C-E
Suites	2 F
Total rooms:	23
Lift	

Restaurant: Closed for Sun
  dinner & Mon lunch (1 Oct
  - Easter only)
Chef: M. Bernard Rigaudis
Prix fixe: Menus at A & B
  A la carte available
Specialities: *Foie de canard cuit
  au sel; Joue de boeuf et oreille
  de porc à la carcassinnaise;
  Cassoulet au confit.*

Seminars: max. 30
Groups: max. 40
Credit cards:
  Access
  American Express
  Diners Club
  Visa
English spoken

Swimming pool
Tennis court

Relais & Châteaux

3km south of Carcassonne and an exit on Autoroute 61. **Airport:** *Carcassonne (3km)*
Station: *Carcassonne (3km)*

This is an imposing, grey-walled, ivy-clad château-hotel with a rather formal atmosphere. Inside, there are long, dimly-lit corridors, uninspiring decorations, vases of plastic flowers, and an occasional piece of modern art which looks rather out of place. The bedrooms are all immaculate with good quality furniture and fittings - although a few are rather small. They are carefully decorated in a rather staid fashion. There is a small bar in the cellar and another more traditional one next to the lounge. The restaurant is the only room with real style. It is on the lower ground-floor, overlooking the terrace and swimming pool. The plain walls are a pretty shade of apricot, the carpets and chairs are beige, and the tables are covered with white over cream. The effect is delightfully harmonious and in striking contrast to the rest of the hotel. The food too is very good (Michelin rosette), making this a place where we'd prefer to eat rather than to stay.

85 CHATEAU DES DUCS DE JOYEUSE H

⚑
11190 Couiza. Aude.
Tel: 68 74 02 80
Propr: The commune of
   Couiza
Direc: Mme Chantal Castillo
Open: All year

Twin with shower   3 B
Double with shower   12 B
Doubles and singles with
   shared w.c. also available
   Total rooms   35
No lift

Mostly for groups. No
   individual bookings July &
   Aug

Restaurant: Open daily
Lunch: 1230
Dinner: 1930
Prix fixe: 1 menu at A
   A la carte available
Demi-pension   B
Specialities: *Cassoulet;*
   Fricassé de Limoux; Salade
   au foie gras et gesiers confits.

Seminars: max. 50
Groups: max. 70
Receptions: max. 150
No credit cards
English & German spoken

Horse-riding
Squash
French courses
Beside river

88km north-west of Perpignan. From there, take the D117 to Quillan. There turn right on to the D118 to Couiza. **Airport:** *Perpignan (84km)* **Station:** *Couiza*

Built in the sixteenth century, this vast stone fortress totally encloses an inner courtyard. During this century, it was used from time to time as a military hospital, a gendarmerie, and a wool store, until eventually it fell into decay. In 1966, the department's agricultural information centre leased the château from the commune of Couiza and undertook a vast restoration project. When this was completed, the château was opened as a place where groups of young people could study and holiday in the countryside. It is, however, open to individuals, except in July and August. The accommodation is rather basic — rather like a youth hostel, but the amenities are good and the charges are extremely low.

86 CHATEAU DE VIOLET H

♥ ♥ ★ ★

Route de Pépieux, 11160
  Peyriac-Minervois, Aude.
Tel: 68 78 10 42
Telex: 505 077 F
Proprs: M. Joseph & Mme
  Emilie Faussié
Open: All year
  (reservations in winter)

Double with bath   16 B-D

No lift. 2 rooms equipped
  for the handicapped.

Restaurant: Open daily
Lunch: 1230 - 1400
Dinner: 1930 - 2300
Prix fixe: Menus A & B
  A la carte available
Specialities: *Canard à toutes les
  sauces; Foie gras à ma façon.*

Demi-pension   B-C

Seminars: max. 25
Groups: max. 30

Credit cards:
  American Express
  Eurocard
  Visa
English spoken

Swimming pool
Tennis court 1km
Horse riding 5km
Golf course 15km

Châteaux Hôtels Indép.
Hostel. du Vignoble Français

25km north-east of Carcassonne (and exit from Autoroute 61). Take the D118 towards Mazamet, but after 5km turn right on to the D620 towards Caunes-Minervois. After 13km turn right on the D11 to Peyriac-Minervois, where turn left on to the D36 towards Pépieux. The château is 1 km further. **Airport:** *Carcassonne (15km)* **Station:** *Carcassonne (15km)*

A Roman villa once stood on this site. The first castle was built there in the eleventh century and was replaced by another four hundred years later. In the mid-nineteenth century, this was demolished and a solid bourgeois residence was built, leaving no traces of the ancient castle. But its legends survive. It is said that, long ago, the daughter of an owner of Château de Violet married a captain in Simon de Montfort's army. On their wedding night, they were both brutally murdered. The funeral was arranged and the grieving mourners assembled. Suddenly, the two corpses sat up in their open coffins and pointed an accusing finger at their murderer — or so the legend states. Even today, when a floor-board creaks or a window rattles it is said to be caused by the young bride's ghost — la Dame Blanche.

But Château de Violet is anything but gloomy. It is in a beautiful position, set amidst a vineyard at the foot of the Black Mountains. The vines which grow right up to the building are used to make a splendid Minervois wine. Inside, much redecoration has recently taken place and all the rooms are very pleasant, especially the dining room, with its large stone fireplace. Most unusually, the bar is decorated with garden furniture that includes a pretty marble fountain mounted on a wall. The bedrooms are all very different in size and style — there is an Empire room, the Archbishop's room, and one with modern Spanish country-furniture. All have a simple charm.

87 CASTEL DE VILLEMAGNE H

♉ ♉ ★ ★
Villemagne, 11310 Saissac, Aude.
Tel: 68 94 22 95
Propr: Colette de Vezian Maksud
Open: 1 March - 31 Oct
  Closed Mon

Twin with shower	2 A
Twin with bath	4 B
Double with bath	2 B
Suite (max. 4)	1 C
Total rooms	9

Restaurant: Closed lunch, except Sat & Sun
Chef: Mme Jeanine Ormierres
Lunch: 1230 - 1300
Dinner: 2000 - 2100
Prix fixe: 3 menus at A
  A la carte available
Specialities: *Cassoulet; Epaule d'agneau farcies.*
Demi-pension (3 days+) B

No lift

Seminars: max. 15
Groups: max. 15
Credit cards
  Eurocard
  Visa

Fishing 500m
Tennis court 7km
Horse riding 10km
Swimming pool 10km

Châteaux Hôtels Indép.

17km north-east of Castelnaudary (where there is an exit from Autoroute 61). Take the D103 towards Saissac. After 16km, turn left on the D34 to Villemagne. **Airport:** *Toulouse (78km)* **Station:** *Castelnaudary (17km)*

The very best atmosphere in a château is created when somehow, the character of the owner and the house are inseparably entwined. This is certainly the case with Castel de Villemagne — a delightful family home in a sleepy village set high in the Black Mountains. The proprietor, Colette de Vezian Maksud, is a personable, straightforward and charming woman who clearly loves her home, which has been owned by her family for generations. Originally built in the fourteenth century, but restructured during the eighteenth, the Castel has a direct, unsophisticated charm that is most appealing.

Throughout the house, there are beautiful pieces of old furniture. Nowhere is overcrowded; nothing is loud or offensive. The bedrooms are all different - large and small; stone-tile and polished wooden floors; some with views of the plain far below, others overlooking the courtyard. Much of the bedroom furniture dates from the end of the nineteenth century, but the rooms are decorated so that they feel light and very agreeable. The dining room is small, with only five tables, but it is very attractive, with crisp white table-cloths, vases of fresh flowers, and pretty

plates. There is a large marble fireplace and terracotta tiles on the floor. An astonishingly wide range of dishes and wines is available. In the large, though rather dark, lounge, there are many games and a collection of books in French on the history and geography of the area. Just across the road from the château is its beautiful ten-acre park.

Far from the normal tourist-beat, Villemagne is a place with a most captiviating, original style where all guests are made extremely welcome.

88 CHATEAU D'ARPAILLARGUES

H

🛡 ★ ★

Arpaillargues, 30700 Uzès Gard.	
Tel: 66 22 14 48	
Telex: 490 415 F	
Propr: M. Gérard Savry	
(Hôtels Particuliers)	
Open: 15 March - 31 Oct	
Twin with bath	9 B-D
Double with bath	18 C-D
Total rooms:	27
No lift	

Restaurant: Closed Wed in
  low season
Prix fixe: Lunch menu at A
  (on weekdays only)
Lunch: 1230 - 1330
Dinner: 1930 - 2100
Specialities: *Petite crêpe de
brandade en aubergine coulis
de tomates; Lasagnes vertes
de saumon; parfait glacé au
zan sauce menthe.*
Demi-pension (3 days+) D-G

Seminars: max. 40
Credit cards:
  American Express
  Diners Club
  Visa
English spoken

Swimming pool
Tennis courts
Horse riding 10km
Golf course 30km
Châteaux Hôtels Indép.

25km north of Nîmes. From there, take the D979 - a beautiful drive - towards Uzès. After 16km, turn left on to the D736, through Blauzac to Arpaillargues. **Airport:** *Nîmes (33km)* **Station:** *Uzès (4km) or Nîmes (25km)*

During the seventeenth and eighteenth centuries, both the château and the village grew together. Now the château — solid and prosperous — is a thriving luxury hotel and much of the village stands empty and deserted.

The hotel was once the home of Marie de Flavigny, Comtesse d'Agoult, who won notoriety by leaving the château and her husband so she could concentrate on being a full-time mistress to Liszt. The house still has reminders of an earlier, more elegant age, including the wide staircase with its iron balustrades and some delightful pieces of antique furniture. But there are some anachronistic touches, like the modern chairs and tables in the main dining room with its gigantic stone fireplace and rough quarry tiles. There are also several satellite dining areas (one, a stone-vaulted hall) and on fine summer evenings it is also possible to dine on the terrace. The food, though from a limited menu, is very good. Fresh fish is the house speciality. The bedrooms are large and well furnished — some having beamed ceilings and quarry-tiled floors. Across a lane, there are attractive grounds with a swimming pool and tennis court. Recommended.

89 CHATEAU DE COULORGUES H

★ ★

Route de Carmignan, 30200
  Bagnols-sur-Cèze, Gard.
Tel: 66 89 57 78, 66 89 54 94
Propr: Mme Aimée Petit
Direc: M. Jean-Pierre
  Grangeon
Open: 1 March - 31 Jan
  Closed Sun eve and Mon
  in low season

No lift. 5 ground-floor
  rooms.

Twin with shower   6 B
Twin with bath   5 B
Double with shower   1 B
Double with bath   11 B
  Total rooms: 23
Restaurant: Closed Sun
  dinner & Mon in low
  season
Chef: M. Jean-Pierre
  Grangeon
Lunch: 1200 - 1400
Dinner: 1930 - 2100
Prix fixe: 3 menus at A
  A la carte available
Demi-pension (3 days+) B-C

Seminars: max. 30
Groups: max. 50
Credit cards:
  Eurocard
  Visa
English, German &
  Spanish spoken

Swimming pool
Tennis court

La Castellerie

33km north of Avignon. From there, take the N100 and, just beyond Villeneuve, turn right on to the N580 to Bagnols-sur-Cèze. At the first round-about, look out for signs to the château and to Carmignan. The road is a small one to the right of the railway-line and before the station. The château is on the right. **Airport:** *Avignon (36km)* **Station:** *Bagnols (nearby)*

Just before the First World War, the original eighteenth-century château on this site was pulled down and replaced with a stone building that has arched windows on the ground floor and a square tower. It is the home of Aimée Petit, a painter, who is now very old. Many years ago she converted into a hotel her château and the disused silk-mill that stood next to it. In the mid-1960s, the mill was destroyed by fire, and a new annexe was built in its place. Mme Petit has handed the management of the hotel over to her chef, Jean-Pierre Grangeon, and his wife. They run an excellent, unpretentious hotel, where the food is superb and the prices are extremely cheap. The well-established grounds are beautiful. Close to the château is a most inviting swimming pool. Not surprisingly, the place is very popular with young couples and family-groups.

Although the interior of the hotel is modern, the public rooms have been furnished and decorated in a pleasing manner. The clean stone-walled dining room, with its large fireplace, has a wrought-iron chandelier and a parquet floor. A large arched window looks out over the vineyard that comes right up to the rear of the building. There is a grey and white Louis XIII-style lounge, with mustard and grey furniture. From the black and white tiled entrance hall, a carpeted stone staircase leads upstairs to the bedrooms in the main building. All are comfortable, though the decorations are mundane. There is one bedroom, decorated all in blue, with an extra-large bed for honeymooners. In the new annexe the bedrooms are small. Those on the ground floor are delightfully cool. The food is the speciality of the hotel and it was most pleasurable dining outside in the shade of the trees by the swimming pool.

90 CHATEAU DE RIBAUTE PG

♛ ♛ ★ ★
30720 Ribaute-les-Tavernes,
Gard.
Tel: 66 83 01 66
Propr: Mme Chamski-
   Mandajors
Open: 1 March - 31 Dec

No lift

Twin with shower   1 A
Double with bath   2 B-C
Suite (max. 4)   1 C
   (inc. breakfast)
Total rooms: 4

Table d'hôte
   (reservation only)   A
Dinner: 2000

Seminars: max 20
No credit cards
English spoken

Swimming pool
Tennis court 1km
Horse riding 2km

Les Etapes François coeur

11km south of Alès. From there, take the N110 towards Montpellier. After 8km, turn right to the village of Ribaute-les-Tavernes. **Airport:** *Nîmes (45km)* **Station:** *Alès (11km)*

Standing in the centre of the village, this lovely old building is listed as an historic monument. It was constructed in the sixteenth century above the cellars of a fourteenth-century fortress that belonged to Odoard de Maubuisson. The château passed into the ownership of the Mandajors in the eighteenth century. During the French Revolution, the house was ransacked and then sold as apartments. The Mandajor family repurchased it, bit by bit, in the early years of the nineteenth century. When the last male heir died fighting for Greek independence, the property passed through the female line until it was inherited by the present owner, Mme Chamski-Mandajors.

The main entrance is north-facing and has a classical facade. A delicate central pediment and corbelled balcony frame the door and window above. Either side of the central block are two large wings that form an attractive courtyard. In the black-and-white tiled entrance hall is a large eighteenth-century stone staircase, with a wrought-iron balustrade that sweeps up and round to the reception rooms above. The pleasant dining room has vaulted stone walls, polished floor tiles and light wooden furniture. The food is very good value. The bedrooms are pleasant and comfortable. Outside, the château is connected to the small village church by an upper exterior passage, which is perfectly conserved. A most interesting place. Recommended.

91 CHATEAU DES CUBIERES H

☗ ★

Route d'Avignon, 30150
  Roquemaure, Gard.
Tel: 66 50 14 28
Propr: The Wagner family
Open: 1 Dec - 15 Nov

Double with shower	3 A-B
Double with bath	17 B
Total rooms	20

No lift

Restaurant (under separate
  management): Closed Tues
Tel: 66 82 89 33
Lunch: 1230 - 1330
Dinner: 1930 - 2100
Prix fixe: Menus at A
Specialities: *Brochettes de
  filets de lapereau au
  poivre vert sur lit de
  pâtes.*
Demi-pension   B

No credit cards in hotel
English spoken

Swimming pool
Fishing 500m
Tennis court 500m
Horse riding 1km

Châteaux Hôtels Indép.

16 north of Avignon. The château is very easy to find, provided you take the correct road. From Avignon, cross the Rhône by the N900 to Villeneuve. (Do NOT take the N100.) Immediately after crossing the river, turn right on to the D980, which winds its way to Roquemaure. The château is on the left, just before the village. **Airport:** *Avignon (21km)* **Station:** *Avignon (16km)*

As this château stands side-on to the nearby main-road, it does not create the best of first impressions. The appearance improves somewhat inside. The spacious entrance-hall is impressive, with a wide sweeping staircase. In the guests' lounge, there is an odd assortment of ornaments, decorations and furniture. The bedrooms vary in size and style. Ours was at the end of the house. It was prettily decorated in a floral pink wallpaper. There was a lacy bedspread and a nylon carpet. Our windows opened on to a small balcony. All seemed fine until night fell. The main road was only a stone's throw away and so we were left with the choice of having the window open and enduring the apparently constant din of traffic or of closing the window and sweltering in the stifling heat. The bath was miniscule and the plumbing exceptionally noisy.

We found the Wagner family polite and their château a reasonably-priced stopping-off place. The restaurant, under different management, is extremely popular, but with only two fixed-price menus the choice is limited.

92 CHATEAU BEAUPRE PG

ᛒ ᛒ ★

Saint-Laurent-des-Arbres,	Double with shower	2 B	No credit cards
30126 Tavel, Gard.	Suites (max. 6)	2 B	English spoken
Tel: 66 50 01 01	(inc. breakfast)		Tennis court 500m
Propr: Mme Berard	Total rooms:	4	Horse riding 4km
Open: All year			Swimming pool 6km
	No restaurant		
No lift			Gîtes de France

20km north of Avignon. From there, cross the Rhône by the N100. At Villeneuve, turn right on to the N580. 13km later there is a road off to the left leading to Saint-Laurent-des-Arbres. Do not take it. On the left, a short way on, is a timber-store. Turn left there, and the lane leads to the château. **Airport:** *Avignon (25km)* **Station:** *Avignon (20km)*

There is such a feeling of dignity and age about this medieval château that it seems almost unreal, as though one had tumbled through a time-warp or on to a realistic, multi-million-dollar film-set. It's not grand; it hasn't been restored; it's very much a family home that happens to be a unique building. Above the entrance to the château is an open gallery, its tiled roof supported by stone pillars atop an ornate stone balustrade. The old oak door is panelled and decorated with metal studs. It leads into a small cobbled central courtyard. Surrounded by covered walkways and galleries it is an entrancing place. Stone steps lead to the bedrooms, with their ancient beams and old furniture. In the vaulted dining room is an enormous chimney with irons and roasting-spit. The sitting-room is also vaulted. Yet here, as throughout the house, there is a strange mixture of modern and antique furniture that marks the place as having been in the family for generations. It has no luxuries, but it has something much rarer - beauty.

93 CHATEAU DE CAILLAN PG

🛡️🛡️🛡️ ★ ★
Caillan, 34550 Bessan,
　Hérault.
Tel: 67 77 42 97, 67 28 27 24
Proprs: M. & Mme Gilbert
　L'Épine
Open: 1 June - 31 Aug

Double with bath　　　2 C
Single with shower　　1 B
　(inc. breakfast)
Total rooms:　　　　　3

No lift

Table d'hôte (res. only)　A

No credit cards
Spanish spoken

Swimming pool
Horse riding
Tennis 10km
Sea 10km

4km south of the Bessan exit from Autoroute 9. 20km east of Bézires, from where, take the D28 to Bessan. In the village, cross over the D13 and, after passing the church, take the small (and only) road that crosses the River Hérault. Immediately afterwards, turn right and that road shortly passes, on the right, the entrance to the château. **Airport:** *Bézires (16km)* **Station:** *Agde (7km)*

We drove to Caillan from Agde, along a narrow unmarked road that wound through miles of vineyards in an apparently deserted countryside. There was no sign-post to show that we'd arrived at the right spot and, from the road, the only sign of the château, was a long avenue of ancient trees running through another vineyard. It led to the back of the château and a large courtyard, around which were also many other buildings used for wine-making. But everywhere looked shuttered and deserted. As we got out of the car, the sun was beating down and a potpourri of delicious scents filled the air. We knocked on the door, but no-one answered. At length we realised that the owners were sensibly lounging round the magnificent swimming pool. Walking through the beautiful garden towards it, we gazed back at the lovely facade of the château. We were surprised to discover that it was not built until 1866, for it has the clean lines and proportions of a fine neo-classical building in the Empire style.

　The château has been in the family of Mme L'Epine since it was built. It is now only a summer residence, for her husband is a busy lawyer. He is, however, also a viticulturist, producing on the estate large quantities of *vin du pays*.

The interior of the house appears to have been little changed since it was built. The hall has a worn but lovely tiled floor; the walls are patterned with the original marbling. In one of the bedrooms, above the French windows which open on to a balcony, is the original ornate pelmet, red with gold-trim. On the landing is a huge portrait of Clemenceau greeting one of Mme L'Epine's ancestors.

This is a delightful château in which to stay. It has all the necessary comforts and conveniences; it is in a beautiful, unspoilt area of France that is close to the coast; and it has charming hosts. It is a perfect opportunity to share in the life of a family château.

94 CHATEAU DE MADIERES H

ŮŮ ★ ★

Madières, 34190 Ganges,
  Hérault.
Tel: 67 73 84 03
Proprs: M. Bernard & Mme
  Françoise Brucy
Open: 24 March - 2 Nov

Twin with shower	2 C
Twin with bath	3 C-D
Double with shower	1 C
Doubel with bath	3 C-D
Suite (max.)	1 D
Total rooms:	10

Restaurant: Open daily
Chef: Mme Françoise Brucy
Lunch: 1200 - 1400
Dinner: 1930 - 2100
Prix fixe: Menus at A & B
A la carte available
Specialities: *Pélardon* (goat-
  cheese) *frit des cévennes;*
  Entrecôte sauce Roquefort;
  Confit de canard.

Groups: max. 20
No lift

Credit cards:
  Eurocard
  Visa
English, German &
  Spanish spoken

By river
Tennis courts 5km
Horse riding 6km
Golf course 30km

Châteaux Hôtels Indép.
Relais du Silence

59km north-west of Montpellier. From there, take the D986 to Ganges, where turn left, across the River Hérault, on to the steep, winding D25 to Madières. The château is in the village at the crossroads with the D48. **Airport:** *Montpellier (64km)* **Station:** *Montpellier (59km)*

This ancient castle is built into a steep side of the Gorges de la Vis. In front of it, its 12-acre estate descends in numerous terraces to the edge of the limpid river below. A document dated 1181 contains the earliest mention of a castle at Madières. In 1326, north and east wings were added. With stout defensive walls on the other two sides, it was then a vast, enclosed and impregnable quadrilateral fortress. In the seventeenth century, part of the outer wall was demolished so that a south wing could be added. It is this wing, with its grand terrace and mullioned windows, that dominates the valley.

  The château was a family home from the time it was built until the beginning of this century. Then it was abandoned and slowly but inevitably fell into decay. In 1983, Bernard and Françoise Brucy bought this magnificent and important historical monument and began the long process of restoration. Now the amazing Château de Madières has been brought back to life. The well appointed rooms and restaurant provide twentieth-century comfort in an ancient setting. From its terrace and bedrooms, the view is splendid. Within easy reach of the hotel are the even more spectacular sights of Le Cirque de Navacelles and La Grotte des Demoiselles.

95 CHATEAU DE LA CAZE H

♥ ♥ ★ ★
La Malène, 48210 Sainte-
  Enimie, Lozère.
Tel: 66 48 51 01
Telex: 490 768 F
Proprs: Mme Simone Roux &
  her daughter, Martine
Open: 1 May - 15 Oct

Twin with bath	10 C-D
Double with bath	4 C-D
Suites (in annexe)	6 D
Total rooms:	20

No lift. 3 ground-floor
  suites.
Restaurant: Closed Tues
Lunch: 1230 - 1400
Dinner: 1930 - 2100
Prix fixe: Menus at B
A la carte available
Specialities: *Ecrevisses*
  (freshwater crayfish);
  *Truite soubeyrane; Foie gras
  chaud; Magret de canard.*
Demi-pension (3 days+) C-D

Seminars: max. 15
Receptions: max. 40
Credit cards:
  American Express
  Diners Club
  Visa

English, German &
  Spanish spoken

Inter. Leading Association

48km north-east of Millau. From there, take the N9. After 7km, turn right on to the D907, which passes through the spectacular Gorge du Tarn. The château is on the right, 5.5km beyond La Malène. **Station:** *Millau (42km)*

The magnificent, legendary Château de la Caze stands on a limestone ledge by the rushing waters of the Tarn, beneath the rugged cliffs of its spectacular gorge. It was Soubeyrane Alamand, the niece of Sainte-Enimie's prior, who first had a castle built at this romantic spot. It was completed in 1489, just in time for her to spend her honeymoon there. A century or so later, the owners were called de Malian and had eight daughters whose beauty is said to have enticed to this remote area all the rich and handsome young men of the time. Their time-aged portraits, painted on wood, now adorn the ceiling of a room in the large south tower. For many years the château stood empty and derelict, but it was converted into a hotel between the two world wars, and since then its beauty and grandeur have continued to attract visitors as successfully as the legendary nymphs of la Caze.

    The castle is a large, grey-stoned, square building with a tower at each corner and above the entrance a lofty keep. Great care has been taken with the interior to preserve a real sense of the building's history. Furnishings and decorations have been selected in a medieval style, and much of the stonework has been left exposed. The restaurant is in the converted chapel. The food, though expensive, is of a high standard (Michelin rosette). Fresh-water fish is the speciality and the old moat is now a well-stocked trout stream.

The bedrooms in the château are spacious, with polished wooden floors and beautiful antiques. Several have large wooden canopied beds. The suites in the annexe are more modern, including huge sunken baths. These rooms are more expensive and it seems a pity to travel so far and not stay in the château itself to savour its romantic and relaxing atmosphere.

96 CHATEAU DE LA MALENE H

Manoir de Montesquiou

♥♥ ★ ★

La Malène, 48210 Sainte-Enimie, Lozère.	Restaurant: Open daily	Credit cards:
	Lunch: 1200 - 1400	Diners Club
Tel: 66 48 51 12	Dinner: 1930 - 2100	Visa
Propr: M. Guillenet	Prix fixe: 2 menus at A	
Open: Easter - 15th Oct	A la carte available	By river
Twin with shower 3 B	Specialities: *Truite à la*	
Twin with bath 4 B	*mousseline de saumon*	Canoeing
Double with bath 3 B	*fumé; Peche du manoir.*	Horse riding 10km
Suite 2 C	Demi-pension B	Swimming pool 20km
Total rooms 12		Tennis court 20km
	No lift	

42km north-east of Millau. From there, take the N9. After 7km, turn right on to the 907, which passes through the spectacular Gorge du Tarn to La Malène. **Station:** *Millau (42km)*

Built of weather-aged stones and half-covered in ivy, this turreted building is a popular tourist hotel (also called Manoir de Montesquiou) at a spectacular part of the Tarn Gorge where two ravines meet. Constructed between the fifteenth and the sixteenth centuries at the base of a steep escarpment, the château seems to grow out of the craggy rocks around it. Much effort has been made to create an authentic atmosphere, with suits of armour, draped fabrics and antique furniture. The dining room is agreeably plain with its white walls and pretty vase of fresh flowers on each table. The food is good and reasonably priced. With cheerful fabrics and interesting period furniture, including four-poster beds, all the bedrooms are comfortable. Each has its own bathroom. A lounge is also available for guests. This is a pleasant, unpretentious and inexpensive place to stay in a beautiful part of France.

97 CHATEAU D'AYRES H

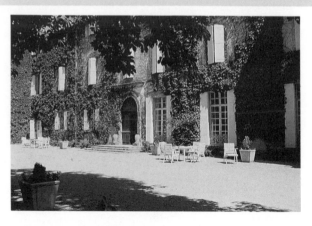

🛡🛡🛡 ★ ★

48150 Meyrueis, Lozère.	Restaurant: Open daily	Seminars max. 15
Tel: 66 45 60 10	Chef: Chantal de Montjou	Groups: max. 30
Propr: Comte Jean-Pierre &	Lunch: 1230 - 1330	Credit cards:
Comtesse Chantal de	Dinner: 1930 - 2130	American Express
Montjou	Prix fixe: Menus at A & B	Diners Club
Open 1 April - 15 Oct	A la carte available	Visa
	Specialities: *Filet de boeuf au*	English & Spanish spoken
Twin with shower 1 B	*roquefort: Confit de canard;*	Tennis court
Twin with bath 10 B-C	*Noisette d'agneau à l'ail doux;*	Horse riding
Double with bath 10 B-C	*Soufflé chaud au Marc*	
Suites (max. 4) 3 C	*d'Alsace.*	Châteaux Hôtels Indép.
Total rooms: 24	Demi-pension B-C	Relais du Silence
No lift.		

42km north-east of Millau. From there, take the N9. After 7km, turn right on to the D907. 14km further, at Le Rozier, turn right on to the D996, through the Gorges de la Jonte, to Meyrueis. Turn right into the village and immediately left to take the D57. The château is a further 1.5km. **Station:** *Millau (42km)*

The road to the château is little more than a farm track that eventually peters out in the mountains of the Cevennes National Park. Hidden behind a high wall in this remote area, Château d'Ayres is now so tranquil that it is hard to imagine that its history has been so tempestuous. It began life as a monastery in the seventh century, but was razed twice before being rebuilt a third time in 1025 for a Benedictine community. It was not until the beginning of the sixteenth century that the monks left, because of the increasing Protestant presence in the area. After the Wars of Religion, the property was taken over by the Galtiers of Montauran, a Protestant family; but not for long. In 1630, the all-powerful Cardinal Richelieu wreaked his revenge and at his command the two towers and the outer wall were demolished. Finally, in the early part of the eighteenth century, the château was again rebuilt, this time as the family home of the Nogarets. They survived there until the beginning of this century, when it was sold and little by little changed into a country inn.

It was, however, only after the château had been purchased by Jean-Pierre and Chantal de Montjou in the late seventies that its reputation was established as a hotel and restaurant. When they took over there were only two guest rooms, now there are twenty-four. All are furnished appropriately, if simply. The arched, white-washed dining room with its stone floors is also a simple room - but the food produced by the Comtesse is first-class. The lounge is a grander place, with a polished wooden floor and some fine antique furniture. Outside, there is a tennis court and, by the terrace, a large circular pond. The château is an ideal base from which to explore the Tarn and Jonte gorges.

98 CHATEAU DE RIELL H

⚓ ★ ★ ★

Molitg-les Bains, 66500
Prades, Pyrénées-
Orientales.
Tel: 68 05 04 40
Telex: 500 705 F
Propr: Mme Biche
Barthélémy
Open: 31 March - 5 Nov

Double with bath   18 E
Suites   3 G
   Total rooms: 21

Lift. 1 ground-floor room.

Restaurant: Open daily
Prix fixe: Menus at B
  A la carte available
Specialities: *Terrine de foie
gras entrelardée de lentilles
à la vinaigrette de truffe;
Crépinette blonde de canette à
la truffe du tricastin; Charlotte
tiède 'Poire Abricot' à la
crème d'amande.*

Seminars max. 100
Groups: max. 40
Credit cards:
  American Express
  Eurocard
  Visa
English spoken
Swimming pools (2)
Tennis courts
Beauty salon & sauna
Lake

Relais & Châteaux

45km west of Perpignan. From there, take the N116 to Prades. In the town, turn right on the D14 to Molitg-les-Bains. **Airport:** *Perpignan (45km)* **Station:** *Prades (7km)*

If you arrive at night, you will not be able to miss Château de Riell. It is as brightly illuminated as any show-ground - and that in a way is what it is. Some of the public rooms are decorated in a style so kitsch that they will either offend or delight - one of the beamed salons has zebra fabric on the walls, the chairs and even the lampshades; coloured lights shining from grilled nooks and crannies in the basement cast strange patterns on the high stone walls; pot-plants and carefully-chosen clutter abound. All very different, the spacious bedrooms are a little more subdued, although the decorations of several bathrooms are unusually exotic.

The exterior of the tall, square, grey-stone château is plain, but its setting is idyllic, being high in the Pyrenees and surrounded by a dense forest of pines and oaks. The views from the bedrooms are spectacular. Numerous facilities are provided for guests, including two swimming pools, a sauna and two tennis courts. The cuisine is excellent and has been awarded a Michelin rosette.

Château de Riell's proprietor, Biche Barthélémy, has with considerable flair given her hotel a style that makes it unusual, perhaps even unique. Highly recommended.

99 CHATEAU DE CIPIERES PG

♥♥♥ ★ ★
06620 Cipières, Alpes-
  Maritimes.
Tel: 93 59 98 00
Telex: 470 395 F
Propr: M. & Mme Capello
  Nerozzi
Open: 1 Dec - 31 Oct

Double with bath	1 C
Suites (max. 4)	6 E-G
(inc. breakfast)	
Total rooms:	7

No lift

Table d'hôte on
  reservation A
Lunch: 1200 - 1400
Dinner: 1930 - 2100
Specialities: *Daube; Agneau et
  raviolis à la provençale.*

Seminars: max. 15
Groups: max. 20

Credit cards:
  American Express
  Diners Club
  Visa
English, German, Italian &
  Spanish spoken.

Swimming pool
Tennis court 100m
Horse riding 400m

La Castellerie
Inter. Leading Association

25km north of Grasse. From there, take the D2085 (towards Nice). After 6km, turn left onto the D3. It's an extremely winding road. After a further 13km, turn left onto the D603 which leads to Cipières. Follow the signs to the chateau's car-park. **Airport:** *Nice (38km)* **Station:** *Cannes (38km) or Nice.*

At an altitude of 750m, this ancient and substantial château dominates the village of Cipières and the beautiful Loup Valley. There was a castle on the site from at least the thirteenth century. Three hundred years later, it fell into the hands of René de Savoie, 'Le Grand Batard'. He and his descendents made the château a bastion of Protestantism. The Catholic Comte de Provence attacked the castle in 1568 and assassinated the occupants. After that, it was occupied by various noble families and in the seventeenth century was completely rebuilt in its present classical form. In 1858, the château was abandoned and from then on local peasants used the vast building as a place to keep their sheep and cattle. In 1951, the Capello family bought the Château de Cipières and began the long process of restoration. In 1989, M. and Mme Capello Nerozzi opened their spectacular home to paying guests.

    The exterior of the building is somewhat austere, but the interior is superb. The rooms are enormous and, in all but those on the third floor, they have high ceilings

with beautifully carved oak beams. Although somewhat smaller, the upper bedrooms are delightful, one having been converted from the pigeonry. Everywhere there are exquisite antiques, magnificent paintings and beautiful tapestries. The bed-linen, with a motif of sprigs of lavender, has been especially designed by Valentino. There is beautiful china and superbly equipped bathrooms. The elegant reception room is in the old library with its ornate furniture and valuable collection of books and manuscripts. There is elaborate carved furniture in the dining room. Everywhere has been decorated and furnished to an extremely high standard. Facilities for guests include a swimming pool, a terrace, a sauna, a jacuzzi and an astronomical telescope. It is an extraordinary place. Strongly recommended.

100 LE CHATEAU EZA H

☺ ★ ★ ★ ♥
06360 Eze Village, Alpes-
  Maritimes
Tel: 93 41 12 24
Telex: 470 382 F
Fax: 93 41 16 64
Propr: M. André Rochat
Open: 1 April - 31 Oct

Twin with bath	7 F-M
Double with bath	2 H-M
Suites (max. 3)	3 K-R
Duplex	1 P
Total rooms:	13

No lift

Restaurant: Open daily
Chef: M. Bruno Cirino
Lunch: 1230 - 1400
Dinner: 1930 - 2230
Prix fixe: Menus at B & C
  A la carte available
Specialities: *Tarte Potagère au
lard croustillant et aux
rouelles de langoustine;
Homard à la concassée de
petits pois et macaronis
truffés; Damier de chocolat
guanaja noir et praliné
amandes de Provence sablées.*

Seminars: max. 10
Credit cards:
  American Express
  Diners Club
  Eurocard
  Mastercard
  Visa
English, German. Italian
  & Spanish spoken

Tennis court 500m
Close to sea
Golf course 6km

12km north-west of Nice. From there, take the N7 to Eze village. Cars have to be left at the 'Relais du Château Eza', which is outside the Castle walls on the Avenue du Jardin Exotique. Coming up the hill, it is 80m after the Mairie on the right. Luggage is either carried by porters or taken up by donkey. Guests have to walk! **Airport:** *Nice (16km)* **Station:** *Nice (12km)*

How do you create from scratch a successful and original hotel? The ingredients are simple enough to record — but exceptionally difficult to find. First of all, you need a fortune that you're willing to spend. Then you must find the perfect location and an ideal building. You need impeccable taste to modernise, decorate, equip and furnish. Finally, you recruit one of France's very best young chefs. That, at least, is how André Rochat set about creating Le Château Eza, and making it one of the most highly praised hotels on the Côte d'Azur.

Le Château Eza is perched on top of a steep cliff, over 1300 feet above the Mediterranean. Part of the magnificent medieval hill-village of Eze, it occupies one of the most attractive sites on the Côte d'Azur. What is now the château was

originally only a collection of disparate, ancient buildings, but in 1920 they were united as a home for Prince William of Sweden. The Swedish royal family sold the property in the early 1950s. In 1976, Andre Rochat, a Swiss citizen, determined to buy it. It was as well that he had been at one time general delegate of the Red Cross in the Middle East for he needed to be a skilled diplomat - six different people owned parts of the château. The delicate negotiations took four years, but in 1980 the purchase was complete.

The intrepid André Rochat then set about converting the château into a small and luxurious hotel. It was 1984 before the hotel was opened - but by then every room and suite was a gem - fine oriental carpets on the floors and the furniture including precious antiques. The restaurant had already been open a year, but it was in 1987 that its reputation was assured when André Rochat brought to Le Château Eza a man who is considered by many to be one of France's best young chefs - Dominique Le Stanc. Now he has moved on. Having sampled the cuisine of his successor, Bruno Cirino, we can report that there has been no decline in the extremely high standards. He is inventive, he uses meticulously selected ingredients, and each dish is immaculately presented. Guests have the choice of dining inside the elegant restaurant or on the balcony, with its panoramic view over the cliffs and sea.

It is, of course, expensive to stay and to dine at Le Château Eza. Although beautifully furnished, the seven double rooms are rather small. Even so, it is one of our favourite hotels in France. It has so many things that are special - the position, the unashamed but unostentatious luxury, the excellence of the cuisine, the perfection of the service (a stole offered to ladies dining on the balcony when the evening becomes slightly chilly), the charm and old-world courtesy of M. Rochat and the special, unique ambience. No wonder that the rich, the famous and the bon-vivants are prepared to leave their cars in the village below and beat a path to the doorstep of Le Château Eza.

101 CHATEAU DE LA CHEVRE D'OR

H

✪ ★ ★ ★

Rue du Barri, 06360 Eze
  Village, Alpes-Maritime.
Tel: 93 41 12 12
Telex: 970 839 F
Fax: 93 41 06 72
Propr: M. Pierre de Daeniken
Open: 1 March - 31 oct

Double with bath   11 F-J
Suites   3 K
  Total rooms: 14

No lift

Restaurant: Open daily
Chef: M. Elie Mazot
Lunch: 1230 - 1400
Dinner: 1930 - 2200
Prix fixe: 1 menu at B
  A la carte available
Specialities: *Fondant de
  courgettes en aumonières de
  saumon; Rougets grillés au
  Chambolle-Musigny; Suprême
  de pigeonneau aux pâtes
  fraiches.*

Credit cards:
  American Express
  Diners Club
  Mastercard
  Visa
English, German, Italian
  & Spanish spoken

Swimming pool
Tennis 500m
Golf course 6km

Relais & Châteaux

12km from Nice. From there, take the N7 to Eze Village. **Airport:** *Nice (18km)* **Station:**
Eze-bord-de-mer (5km)

'For more than a thousand years, this majestic château has stood ...' So start many
potted descriptions of this hotel. It is true that the Village d'Eze was an ancient
settlement and that a medieval château existed there, but it was destroyed in 1806
on the order of Louis XIV, who wanted to restrict the power of its owner, the
Comte de Nice. It was not until 1920 that the celebrated American violinist,
Balakovic, decided to reconstruct the château on the original site. Several reasons
are given as to why he called it 'Le Château de la Chèvre d'Or' — in memory of
a goat that used to wander through the streets or because of an ancient golden
statuette found on the site. Whatever the reason for the name, it became one of

the most famous on the Côte d'Azure after the château was transformed into a hotel and restaurant in 1953 by Bruno Ingold, who, like the owner of Le Château Eza, was an ex-Swiss diplomat. Early in 1989, M. Ingold died and the hotel was taken over by M. Pierre de Daeniken.

There are only fourteen bedrooms in this mock-medieval château. Some are rather small, but all have spectacular views and are luxuriously furnished. It is, however, the panoramic restaurant for which La Chèvre d'Or is most renowned. The long-established chef, Elie Mazot, with considerable flair produces a combination of nouvelle and traditional cuisine that satisfies the adherents of both (one Michelin rosette and two Gault Millau red toques). Its cheese-board had one of the best selections we've seen in France.

In front of the hotel is a terrace, a delicious garden full of exotic flowers, and two small swimming pools. With the spectacular views, it is a perfect place to relax. The hotel and restaurant are extremely popular with the rich and famous. Reservations are essential and not always easy to obtain.

102 CHATEAU DU DOMAINE SAINT-MARTIN H

♛ ♛ ★ ★ ♟

Route de Coursegoules,
06140 Vence,
Alpes-Maritimes.
Tel: 93 58 02 02
Telex: 470 282 F
Fax: 93 24 08 91
Propr: the Geneve family
Direc: Mlle Andrée Brunet
Open: 15 March - 15 Nov

Double with bath	14 H-L
Suites	11 N-Q
Total rooms:	25

No lift. 2 ground-floor
rooms.

Restaurant: Open daily
Chef: M. Dominique Ferrière
Lunch: 1230 - 1400
Dinner: 1930 - 2100
Prix fixe: Menus at B & C
A la carte available
Specialities: *Fricassée de ris
de veau aux langoustines;
Filets d'agneau en croûte de
sel aux herbes; Feuilleté aux
fraises des bois.*

Seminars: max. 15
Groups: max. 15
Receptions: max. 50
Credit cards:
American Express
Diners Club
Visa
English, German & Italian
spoken

Swimming pool
Tennis court
Golf course 20km

Relais & Châteaux

*25km north-west of Nice. From there, take the N98 — the coastal road. At Cagnes-sur-Mer,
just before the race-course, turn right on the Boulevard J.F. Kennedy. Follow the one-way
system through Cagnes-Ville and then turn right into Avenue de Verdun to take the D36
to Vence. There turn right on the D2 towards Coursegoules. The château is a further 2.5km,
on the left.* **Airport:** *Nice (18km)* **Station:** *Nice (25km)*

This expensive hotel provides every luxury in a perfect setting. Standing high in
the hills above Vence, the thirty-acre estate of Saint-Martin presents a spectacular
panorama of the whole Riviera from Cap Ferrat to Antibes. Since Roman times,

there has been a fortified stronghold on the site. In 1115, the Count of Provence handed over the estate to the crusaders returning from Jerusalem on condition that they protected the region and cultivated the land. The Knights of the Temple established a community on the site, but in 1307, King Philippe IV accused the Templars of witchcraft and burnt its leaders. He did not, however, find their treasure and the legend persists that it is still buried on the site. When M. Geneve bought the estate in 1936, the bill of sale stated that 'in the event of the treasure being found, it shall be shared amongst the assignee and the previous owner'.

The château, as it exists today, was built by M. Geneve on the ruins of the Templars' castle, although the old drawbridge and tower still survive. In all the spacious bedrooms and public areas there are beautiful antiques and oriental carpets. On the walls is a fine collection of modern paintings and wonderful flower arrangements decorate the long marbled halls. In addition to the main house, small villas (called 'bastides')

are set in the terraces among the dense olive groves. These are the luxurious suites. The restaurant is famed throughout the area and boasts a Michelin rosette. The chef, Dominique Ferrière, provides rich, traditional fare using the fresh produce of the extensive estate. We consider the food at Saint Martin to be among the best served in any château-hotel.

But the most impressive thing about Saint Martin is the staff and the extremely able director, Mlle Brunet. As soon as guests arrive, they're made to feel at home. The service is of that highest standard found only in a top-quality hotel. Every evening, beds are prepared, shutters closed, clothes put away, and the room left immaculate. The staff in the dining room, including several who have been at Saint Martin for over twenty years, are extremely knowledgeable and helpful. A magnificent, albeit expensive, luxury hotel. Most highly recommended.

103 MAS DE LA BRUNE H

♕ ♕ ♕ ★ ★ ♥
13810 Eygalières-en-Provence,
  Bouches-du-Rhone.
Tel: 90 95 90 77
Telex: 771 992 F
Fax: 90 95 99 21
Propr: Sarl Mas de la Brune
Direc: M. Stefan H. Gagg
Open: 6 April - 1 Nov

Demi-pension only
Twin with bath   4 D
Double with bath   4 D
Double with bath   5 D
Suite   1 D
  (inc. demi-pension)
  Total rooms: 10
No lift

Restaurant: Closed Tues &
  Wed lunch
Chef: M. Alain Frontier
Lunch: 1200 - 1300
Dinner: 1930 - 2100
Prix fixe: Menus at B
  A la carte available
Specialities: *Oeufs brouillés
  au poisson fumé; Suprême de
  rascasse à la badiane étoilée et
  à la verveine; Magret de
  canard des landes au poivre
  vert et zeste d'orange; Saboyan
  au champagne aux fruits
  rouges.*

Credit cards:
  American Express
  Eurocard
  Visa
English, German and Italian
  spoken

Swimming pool
Golf course 15 km

Inter. Leading Association
La Castellerie

27km south-east of Avignon. From there, take the N7 (towards Salon-de-Provence). After 18km, at Saint-Andiol, turn right onto the D24. After 5.5km, cross over the D99 onto the D74A to Eygalières. Carry on through the village and shortly afterwards the château is on the right. **Airport:** *Marseille (35km)* **Station:** *Orgon (9km)*

Constructed in 1572 by Pierre Isnard, Mas de la Brune is an important example of French Renaissance architecture. The most attractive facade of gleaming white stone has mullioned windows on the first floor. At the upper corner of the facade is a corbelled, circular watchtower with an elaborately decorated dome. Beneath the tower is an angled niche, surmounted by a triangular pediment supported by two ornamental columns. Standing in the niche is the statue of a mermaid holding a fish. Above the arched central door is a decorative cartouche that probably contained a coat of arms before it was mutilated during the Revolution. Immediately inside the door is the original spiral staircase with its time-worn steps. On its central stone column is a stone-coping carved with four heads — two of angels and two with grotesque faces, one representing gluttony and the other anger.

For a number of years, this beautiful Provençal château has been a hotel. After several changes of ownership and a period of decline, it was fully refitted and redecorated at the beginning of 1989 and reopened as a small but impressive first-class hotel. All the bedrooms are immaculately decorated, usually with a predominant colour such as deep blue or a rich russet. Some of the beds are four-posters and most of the furniture is high-quality antiques. The first-floor bedrooms have elaborately beamed ceilings. On the floors, there are old glazed tiles, covered with oriental rugs. The bathrooms are excellent. Downstairs, there is a fascinating fan-vaulted lounge, with stone-flag floors and a vast open fireplace. Comfortably furnished with beautifully upholstered wooden-framed chairs and a matching heavily-padded settee, it is a wonderful place to relax after an evening meal. And

the food at Mas de la Brune is excellent - among the very best we have tasted at a château-hotel. (It's just as well. Guests are really obliged to eat there, as only demi-pension is available at the hotel.) The chef, Alain Frontier, was previously responsible for the much-lauded cuisine at Château de la Caze. Although in summer guests may prefer to dine on the attractive terrace in the shade of centuries-old plane trees, the dining room is a spectacular place with its smooth arched roof and ancient olive-press embedded in the massive stone of an end wall. Whether inside or out, the tables are most elegantly laid, with crisp pink table-cloths and naperies and pretty china. The wine-list is impressive — the hotel boasts an air-conditioned wine-cellar where over a hundred and thirty vintage French wines are stored. A special - and unusual - word of praise must be given to the lighting throughout Mas de la Brune. While being discreet and unobtrusive, it is both efficient and does much to help create the special ambience present throughout the hotel.

A great deal is done for the well-being of guests. The gates at the end of the long drive are kept locked and a bell has to be rung before they are opened. At night, cars are kept in a locked compound. It is a non-smoking restaurant. Towelling dressing-gowns are provided for guests wishing to use the large outdoor swimming pool. The atmosphere at Mas de la Brune is extremely relaxed — much more like being in someone's elegant country home than in an hotel. The director at Mas de la Brune is Stefan Gagg, who hails from Switzerland. Attentive, affable, extremely efficient and hard-working, he is undoubtedly responsible for much of Mas de la Brune's new success. Strongly recommended.

104 CHATEAU DE MEYRARGUES H

♕ ♕ ★ ★

13650 Meyrargues, Bouches-du-Rhone.
Tel: 42 57 50 32
Proprs: M. Valérie Ferrand
& M. Gaston Flaud
Open: 1 March - 15 Jan

Twin with bath	12 D-F
Double with bath	3 D-E
Suites (max. 5)	3 H
Total rooms:	18

No lift

Restaurant: Closed Mon in
  low season
Chef: M. Jean-Luc L'Hourre
Lunch: 1200 - 1430
Dinner: 2000 - 2200
Prix fixe: Menus at B
  A la carte available
Demi-pension (2 days+) D

Seminars: max. 25
Groups: max. 30
Receptions: max. 120
Credit cards:
  American Express
  Visa
English, Italian &
  Spanish spoken

Inter. Leading Association
La Castellerie

Close to exit 15 on Autoroute 51. 11km north of Aix-en-Provence, from where take the N96 to Meyrargues. The château is on a hill dominating the village and is well signposted.
Airport: *Aix-en-Provence (17km)* **Station:** *Aix-en-Provence (11km)*

This ancient castle stands proudly and defiantly on a hill overlooking central Provence. Since its construction in the Middle Ages, it has been the home of many French nobles, including the Comte de Provence and Queen Yolande, the widow of Louis II. It became a hotel in 1952. At the beginning of 1989, the château was acquired by new owners: Valérie Ferrand, who was an interior designer in Paris, and Gaston Flaud, who was her bank manager — a useful combination of previous occupations for the expensive task of carrying out much needed renovations to a vast château-hotel. They have undertaken the task with enthusiasm. New rooms have been created and the old ones have been redecorated with attention to detail. Around each bed is a drapery of attractive fabric with a modern design. There are dried flower arrangements in each room and some nice pieces of furniture. All the bathrooms are brand-new and well equipped. The vaulted dining room with its glazed-tile floor is a pleasant place to eat and the food is of a high standard. There is a large lounge with a heavily beamed ceiling and a massive stone open fire-place.

Enclosed by the ancient, honey-coloured stone exterior of the château, there is a splendid terrace with a most impressive view.

105 CHATEAU DES ALPILLES H

♛ ♛ ★ ★

Ancienne Route du Grès,
  13210 Saint-Rémy-de-
  Provence, Bouches-du-
  Rhône.
Tel: 90 92 03 33
Telex: 431 487 F
Proprs: Mme Françoise &
  Mlle Catherine Bon
Open: 1 March - 3 Jan

Lift. 1 ground-floor room.

Twin with bath	9 D-E
Double with bath	7 D-E
Suites	1 F
Total rooms:	17
Apartment	1

Poolside grill (lunch only) A

Seminars: max. 25
Groups: max. 17

Credit cards:
  American Express
  Diners Club
  Eurocard
  Visa
English spoken

Swimming pool
Tennis courts

Châteaux Hôtels Indép.

25km north-east of Arles. From there, take the N570. After 13km, turn right towards Saint-Rémy on the D32 (which at Saint-Etienne joins the D99). At Mas-Blanc-des-Alpilles, turn right onto the narrow D31. The château is a further 6km on the left. **Airport:** *Avignon (35km)* **Station:** *Avignon (25km)*

Ancient plane trees line the drive and cast dappled shadows over the attractive facade of this early nineteenth-century château. Once the home of one of the oldest families in Arles, the Pichots, it was visited by many politicians and writers, such as Châteaubriand, Lamartine, Guizot and Thiers. It has been a hotel for some years and the attractive grounds are dominated by the amenities provided for the guests — the two tennis courts, and a luxurious swimming pool with its shady bar. A tiny brook gurgles across the lawn and through the magnificent trees.

The château interior is a mixture of the old and new. There are gold-painted rococo ceiling decorations and arrangements of plastic flowers, displays of medieval armour and comfortable modern furniture. The ornate salon, with its elaborate gilded ceiling, gilt-framed mirror and intricate mosaic floor, has a suite of Louis XIV furniture — although it is a room that seems designed more for effect than use. The breakfast room is also ornate, with modern white plastic furniture and a nineteenth-century floor-to-ceiling painting on each wall depicting the four seasons.

A huge tapestry dominates the tiled stairs and landing. The bedrooms are faultless. Decorated with admirable restraint, furnished with antiques, fully-carpeted and with luxurious bathrooms, they are all superb. Attention has been given to small, but important details: there is mosquito netting at the windows and towelling robes to wear down to the pool. Smaller and much cheaper bedrooms are available on the second floor for children or accompanying staff. In converted buildings in the grounds there is an ultra-modern, delightful flat and two holiday apartments.

The hotel does not have a restaurant, although salads and grills are available at the poolside. There is also a comprehensive room service. The hotel is most efficiently run by Mlle Bon, and every help is given to guests. Highly recommended.

106 CHATEAU DE ROUSSAN H

♥ ♥ ★ ★
Route de Tarascon, 13210
  Saint-Rémy-de-Provence,
  Bouches-du-Rhône.
Tel: 99 92 11 63
Propr: Miss Catherine E.
  McHugo
Open: 21 March - 20 Oct

Twin with shower	1 C
Twin with bath	3 C-E
Double with bath	8 C-E
Total rooms:	12

No lift. 1 ground-floor room.

Restaurant: Open daily

Credit cards:
  Visa
English spoken

Spring-water pool
Tennis 2km

25km north-east of Arles. From there, take the N570. After 13km, turn right towards Saint-Rémy on the D32 (which at Saint-Etienne joins the D99). The château is on the right, 2km before Saint-Rémy. **Airport:** *Avignon (35km)* **Station:** *Avignon (25km)*

Château de Roussan is approached by a long tree-lined avenue that is the most beautiful we saw anywhere in the south of France. At the end of the long tunnel of dense foliage, barely pierced by thin beams of sun-light, visitors can see a small part of the château's imposing facade. As they approach closer, more and more is unveiled, until at last the great dignity and presence of the noble building can be fully seen. Yet this is not an ostentatious château. It was built at the beginning of the eighteenth century — a golden age of château design and construction when the bold simplicity of line and the perfection of proportion were more important than flamboyant ornamentation. The entrance is at the back, where a shingled courtyard is alive with the soothing murmur of running water. A spring-fed brook runs throughout the utterly delicious garden. Clear and icy, it flows first into a pool that is flanked by weather-aged stone statues. From there, it meanders down to the courtyard where it spouts out into ornate stone basins full of gold-fish and then on into a long tree-covered and trout-filled canal beside the château.

    In 1989, the château was acquired by Catherine McHugo, the successful proprietor of the nearby Domaine de Valmouriane. Many changes have been made — a restaurant has been introduced, rooms have been redecorated and the old antique furniture has been replaced. Time will tell whether these have been improvements to what — under the previous management — was one of our favourite châteaux-hotels.

107 ABBAYE DE SAINTE CROIX H

♥♥ ★ ★ ★
Route de Val-de-Cuech,
  13300 Salon, Bouches-du-
  Rhône.
Tel: 90 56 24 55
Telex: 401 247 F
Propr: The Bossard family
Direc: Catherine Bossard
Open: 1 March - 2 Nov
Twin with shower   1 C
Twin with bath   8 C-E
Double with shower   2 C-E
Double with bath   9 C-E
Suites (max. 4)   4 E-H
   Total rooms: 24
No lift. 5 ground-floor
  rooms.

Restaurant: Closed Mon
  lunch
Chef: Yves Sauret
Lunch: 1230 - 1400
Dinner: 1930 - 2100
Prix fixe: Menus at A-C
  A la carte available
Specialities: *Gambas flambées et
  compotée de fenouil au beurre
  de pastis; Escalope de loup à
  l'huile de basilic; Noisettes
  d'agneau et jus de truffes
  noires.*

Seminars: max. 50
Groups: max. 50
Receptions: max. 150
Credit cards:
  Diners Club
  Mastercard
  Visa
English & German spoken

Swimming pool
Tennis court 200m
Golf course 25km

Relais & Châteaux

46km south-east of Avignon. From there, take the N7 (towards Aix-en-Provence). After 34km, at Senas, turn left on the N538 to Salas. At the entry to the town, turn left onto the ring-road and then turn left onto the D16. This passes under the A7, and 3km further there is a right turn leading to the abbey. **Airport:** *Istres-le-Tube (24km)* **Station:** *Salon (5km)*

From time immemorial, Sainte-Croix was a religious site. Hermit cells existed in the cliff there long before Saint Hilaire, after his return from Palestine, founded the chapel of Notre-Dame de Cuech, donating to it, according to legend, a piece from Christ's cross. The Roman walls were built during the sixth century and during the Middle Ages, the abbey became one of the most famous and most visited in the south of France. In 1791, during the Revolution, the abbey was sold. It was briefly re-established as a religious house during the First Empire of Napoleon I, but in 1826 it was abandoned and slowly fell into ruins. A massive earthquake in 1909 caused considerable damage. In 1960, the Bossard family acquired the abbey and began the slow, meticulous process of restoration.

The work complete, there is now at Sainte-Croix an impressive collection of buildings set in grounds of forty-five acres. The court of the beautiful twelfth-century Roman chapel, with its four vaulted bays and choir, leads through a Renaissance portico into an enclosed courtyard surrounded by the smaller buildings that have been converted in a spectacular and most unusual hotel of great comfort. Most of the floors have beautiful, polished square tiles. There are vaulted ceilings in many of the rooms, including bedrooms and the large lounge with its monumental open fireplace. Outside the dining room, there is a tree-shaded terrace with views across the plain all the way to the sea. Everywhere is well furnished, with many antiques and ancient artifacts. The food is excellent. The swimming pool is delightful. A very special place.

108 CHATEAU D'ENTRECASTEAUX

PG

🛡️🛡️🛡️ ★ 🍷

83570 Entrecasteaux, Var	Twin with bath	2 D-E	Credit cards:
Tel: 94 04 43 95	Double with bath	1 E	American Express
Propr: M. Lachlan McGarvie-	Total rooms:	3	English, German & Spanish
Munn			spoken
Open: All year	No restaurant		Small swimming pool
			Tennis court 500m
No lift	Seminars: max. 25		
			Château Accueil

*27km north-east of the exit from the A 8 at Brignoles. From there, take the D954 to La Val,
where turn right on the D562 through Carcès. 3km further, turn left on the narrow D31
to Entrecasteaux.* **Airport:** *Hyères (73km)* **Station:** *Brignoles (27km)*

Perched on a rock above a tiny medieval village, this imposing château dates back
to the eleventh century, although the existing building was constructed between
the sixteenth and the seventeenth centuries. A long, thin, three-storeyed building,
it has at various times been the home of some of the most illustrious and notorious
men of Provence: François Adhemar de Castellane who in 1669 was appointed
Lieutenant-General of Provence; Marquis Raymond de Bruny d'Entrecasteaux,
Treasurer General of France; and the man who blackened the name of his family
and village, Marquis Jean-Baptiste Bruny d'Entrecasteaux, President for life of the
Parliament of Provence who, on 30 May 1784, murdered his young wife and fled
to Portugal. By the intervention of the parish priest, the château escaped the
ravages of the mob during the French Revolution and remained in the hands of
descendents of the Brunys until 1949, when it was bought by the municipality of
Entrecasteaux. Unfortunately, there was neither the staff nor the money to
maintain the building — the furniture and paintings were sold, important books
and documents disappeared, and eighteenth century walnut woodwork was used
for fire-wood. In 1974, the painter Ian McGarvie-Munn purchased the still
impressive but vandalised château from the municipality. He and later his son,
Lachlan, dedicated themselves to the task of restoring and revitalising this
important historic monument.

And how magnificently they have accomplished the task. Not only have the furnishings and fittings created an interior of impressive beauty, but the many salons have become centres for the cultural and social life of the community. Held there are weddings and receptions, concerts and recitals, exhibitions and events. It is little wonder that the restoration work has been awarded so many prizes, including in 1980 the Obelisque du Conseil de l'Europe, in 1986 the Prix de la Fondation Americaine and in 1989 the Label du Meilleur Accueil, awarded by the Ministry of Tourism. Outside, the garden, which was designed by the famous landscape artist, Le Nôtre, and now belongs to the community, has been restored to its former, formal beauty.

Only three rooms are available for guests. The most spectacular of these is La Chambre de la Marquise with its incredible, palatial marble bathroom. There are two other more modern but extremely comfortable, white, bright rooms on the second floor. Both have excellent bathrooms. Lachlan McGarvie-Munn and Andréa, his wife, are a cultured, generous and hospitable couple who make staying in their home, Château d'Entrecasteaux, a rare and delightful pleasure. Most strongly recommended.

109 DOMAINE DE CHATEAUNEUF

H

♥ ♥ ★ ★ ★
83869 Nans-les-Pins, Var.
Tel: 94 78 90 06
Telex: 400 747 F
Propr: Mme Jeanne Malet
Direc: M. Gilbert Duval
Open: 1 April - 30 Nov

Twin with shower	4 C
Twin with bath	7 D
Double with shower	3 C
Double with bath	12 D
Suites (max. 3)	6 F-T
Total rooms:	32

No lift

Restaurant: Closed Mon in
 low season
Chef: M.M. Allemann
Lunch: 1230 - 1400
Dinner: 2000 - 2130
Prix fixe: Menus at A & B
 A la carte available
Specialities: *Foie gras de
canard traité par le chef;
Filet de truite de mer au
coulis de langoustine;
Poêlée de laperau sautée
aux olives et dragées d'ail
confites à la barigoule de
petits legumes.*
Demi-pension (3 days+) C

Seminars: max. 25
Groups: max. 25
Credit cards:
 American Express
 Diners Club
 Eurocard
 Visa
English & German spoken

Swimming pool
Tennis courts
Golf course
Helipad

Relais & Châteaux

42km east of Aix-en-Provence. From there, take the N7 (or the A8) to Saint-Maximin-la-Sainte-Baume, where turn right onto the N560. At a major junction, where the D1 starts on the left, continue on the N560. The entrance to the château is a further 500m on the left. **Airport:** *Marseille (64km)* **Station:** *Marseille (41km)*

The opening of the 18-hole Sainte-Baume golf course, right next to this château, has made it even more popular. It already possessed excellent facilities for guests, including a swimming pool and three tennis courts.

 Built at the beginning of the eighteenth century on a pilgrim-way, the exterior is plain but attractive. Inside is delightful. There is a lot of antique furniture and carpets, but nothing as rare or impressive as the original hand-painted wall-hangings, which after 200 years are still on the walls of the sitting-room. They depict in delicate colours delightful pastoral scenes. Rooms vary in price according to their size, but all are well furnished, simply but elegantly decorated, and extremely comfortable. The hotel is most ably managed and has a willing and cheerful staff.

Domaine de Chateauneuf (109)

110 CHATEAU DE FERLANDE PG

♦ ♦ ★

Route de Saint-Côme, 83270
Saint-Cyr-sur-Mer, Var.
Tel: 94 26 29 17
Propr: Mme Roselyne
Contencin
Open: 1 May - 31 Oct

Double with bath   1 C
Suites (max. 3)   2 D
Total rooms: 3

No lift

No restaurant

No credit cards
English spoken

Beach & marina 2km

Château Accueil

24km north-west of Toulon. From there, take the D559. 6.5km beyond Bandol (and 1.5km before Saint-Cyr), turn right onto the narrow D266 towards La Cadière. The long drive to the château is 500m on the left. **Airport:** *Hyères (44km)* **Station:** *Saint-Cyr or Bandol (8km)*

In an area that claims to have three hundred and twenty days of sunshine every year, this elegant Provençal château of the eighteenth century, with its clean white walls and shuttered windows, is set in an agreeable tree-shaded garden. All around are the vineyards from which the famous Bandol red wine is produced. Outside the château, there is a stepped terrace, edged with neat box hedges. Inside has been entirely restored in keeping with the styles and tradition of the period. Very much a private home, there are available for paying guests only two well furnished and comfortable apartments and a double room. With such limited accommodation, reservations are essential.

Château de Ferlande is in a pretty, quiet spot, close to several medieval villages, including Le Castellet. Yet it is only 2km away from the nearest beach. Within easy access is all the hubbub of life on the French Riviera, including the international race-track near Le Castellet.

111 CHATEAU DE TRIGANCE H

♜ ★ ★

83840 Trigance, Var.
Tel: 94 76 91 18
Propr: M. Jean-Claude
  Thomas
Open: 20 March - 31 Oct

Twin with bath	4 C
Double with bath	4 C
Suites (max. 3)	2 D
Total rooms	10

No lift

Restaurant: Closed Wed (in
  low season)
Chef: M. Laurent Ollier
Lunch: 1200 - 1400
Dinner: 1930 - 2100
Prix fixe: Menus at A & B
  A la carte available
Specialities: *Foie gras de canard
  et sa sauce tiède au loupiac;
  Casserolette de filets de sole
  au corail d'oursins.*
Demi-pension   C

Credit cards:
  American Express
  Diners Club
  Eurocard
  Visa
English spoken

Tennis court 500m
Swimming pool 20km

Relais & Châteaux

*42km north of Draguignan. From there, take the D955 through Comps-sur-Artuby. After
a further 9km, turn left on the D90 to Trigance, where a road to the right leads to the
château.* **Airport:** *Hyères (80km)* **Station:** *Les Arcs (54km)*

This is yet another example of a ruined medieval fortress that has been lovingly
restored in recent years. Its origins date back to the ninth century, when a fortress
was built on the steep pinnacle overlooking the Verdon river as a place of
meditation for the monks of Saint Victor of Marseille. In the thirteenth century, it
became a nobleman's castle and remained so until it was destroyed during the
French Revolution. As with most castles that met the same fate, its stones were
used to build many houses in the area. In 1961, having fallen in love with the place,
M. Hartmann purchased the ruin with the intention of rebuilding it as a hotel. It
was an enormous undertaking. Ten years later, the property was acquired by M.
and Mme Thomas, who continued the work.

   With the stone walls of Trigance constantly visible like a brooding eagle perched
atop a rocky crag, the narrow approach road winds up behind the castle till it ends
at a car-park. After that, guests have to walk up a steep path which, when we
breathlessly counted them, contained eighty-five steps. Entering the castle is
somewhat of a disappointment. There is surprisingly little there, considering the

vastness of the exterior walls. The dining room is cave-like, with windowless, rough stone walls and an arched ceiling, heavily encrusted with jagged pieces of rock. The efforts to create a medieval atmosphere are somewhat spoiled by modern furniture and rather twee effects - painted shields and banners that seem to be left-overs from an amateur Gilbert and Sullivan production. However, several guests we spoke to loved it. The bedrooms and bathrooms are good. Some have four-poster beds with crenellated canopies. There is a small terrace with a spectacular view. The best things about Trigance are the helpfulness of the staff, including M. Thomas, and the food, which is very good, especially the desserts.

112 CHATEAU LES LONNES H

★ ★ ★
Vieux Chemin de Moulins
    d'Entraigues, 83550
    Vidauban, Var.
Tel: 94 73 65 76
Telex: 460 016 F
Propr: M. Eric & Mme Lisa
    Trepp
Open: All year

Twin with bath	6 D-G
Double with bath	6 D-G
Suites	2 G-M
(inc. breakfast)	
Total rooms:	14
Lift	

Restaurant: Open daily
Lunch: 1200 - 1400
Dinner: 1900 - 2100
Prix fixe: Menus at A & B
    A la carte available
Specialities: *Mousseline de
    rascasse et son coulis
    d'oursins; Tian de Saint-
    Jacques au beurre de
    Champagne; Carré d'agneau
    du moulin des iscles;
    Aiguillettes de canard au
    vinaigre de zérès et miel;
    Filet de boeuf Magdalene.*

Seminars: max. 20
Receptions: max. 50
Credit cards:
    American Express
    Visa
English, German, Italian &
    Spanish spoken

Tennis court
Swimming pool
Sauna
Solarium
Golf course 15km

Châteaux Accueil
Inter. Leading Association

10km from the Le Luc exit on the A8 and 69km north-east of Toulon. From there, take the A57, which turns into the N97. Continue on this to Le Luc, where it joins the N7. Turn right on this to Vidauban. Just before entering the village, turn left on the narrow D64. The château is a further 3km. **Airport:** *Toulon (71km)* **Station:** *Vidauban (4km)*

Built in the eighteenth century, this isolated building was originally used for growing silk worms. Standing in its own grounds of over fifty acres, Château Les Lonnes is now a first-class hotel run by Eric and Lisa Trepp. All the refurbishment has been done to the highest standard. The comfortable bedrooms have beamed wooden ceilings, fitted carpets, good quality wooden furniture and mosquito-netting at the windows. The marble-tiled bathrooms are superb. There are several salons for guests, including one with a large stone open-fireplace. The inventive cuisine of the chef, Patrick Schwartz, is most agreeable. Both the dining rooms are extremely pleasant - one has glazed-tile floors and a large brick archway, while the other is on an enclosed terrace, overlooking the large swimming pool. In addition to the more sporting provisions, there is also an 'English' bar and a Vinothèque, where wines from Provence can be sampled and bought.

113 HOSTELLERIE CHATEAU DES FINES ROCHES H

⚑ ★ ★
84230 Châteauneuf-du-Pape,
  Vaucluse.
Tel: 90 83 70 23
Proprs: M. Henri Estevenin
Open: 1 Feb - 20 Dec, but
  closed Sun evenings &
  Mon, except high season

Twin with shower	2 C
Twin with bath	3 D
Double with bath	2 C
Total rooms:	7

No lift

Restaurant: Closed Mon
Chefs: M. Pierre & M.
  Philippe Estevenin
Lunch: 1200 - 1400
Dinner: 1900 - 2100
Prix fixe: 1 menu at B
  A la carte available
Specialities: *Terrine de foie
  gras et sa brioche aux raisins;
  Filet de boeuf au Châteauneuf-
  du-Pape; Chariot de desserts,*

Demi-pension (2 days+) E

Seminars: max. 25
Groups: max. 12
Credit cards:
  Eurocard
  Visa
English, German, Italian &
  Spanish spoken

Les Cuisiniers et Hôteliers
  de Métier

12km south of Orange (and the exit junction of Autoroutes 7 and 9). From the town centre, take the D68 to Châteauneuf-du-Pape. There, turn left on the D192 towards Bedarrides. The château is 2km further on the right. **Airport:** *Avignon (22km)* **Station:** *Orange (12km)*

This creeper-covered, crenellated mock-medieval fort, built in the nineteenth century, is surrounded by the famous Châteauneuf-du-Pape vineyards. The hostellerie occupies part of the château. There is a slightly stuffy feel about the place with its mock-medieval appearance (mounted animal horns on the walls, tapestries and dark furniture). The bedrooms vary in size and appear comfortable. However, at the hostellerie, the food's the thing, not the accommodation or, for that matter, the decor. Its cuisine, under the direction of the owner's sons, Pierre and Philippe, has justifiably won fame, including a Michelin rosette. The food is good (especially the desserts) and is very reasonably priced. There are two restaurants. 'Grand Calme Panorama' is the posh one - there is another that is more modest (but the prices and the food are the same). The restaurant is strongly recommended.

In another part of the château are the wine-caves of the renowned Louis Mousset. They are certainly well worth a visit.

Index of Chateaux

RIELL - Molitg-les-Bains 98
RIGNY - Rigny 35
ROCHEGUDE - Rochegude 73
ROMEREL - Saint-Valery-sur-Somme 15
ROUSSAN - Saint-Rémy-de-Provence 106

SAINT-GERMAIN-DU-PLAIN - Saint-Germain-du-Plain 50
SAINT-HUBERT - Hallines 3
SAINT-JEAN - Parc Saint-Jean 58
SAINT-MARTIN - Vence 102
SAINTE CROIX — Salon 107
SAMPZON - Sampzon 70
SAULON-LA-RUE - Saulon-la-Rue 39

THOIRY - Thoiry-en-Yvelines 24
TILQUES - Tilques-Saint-Omer 6
TRIGANCE - Trigance 111

URBILHAC - Lamastre 68

VALOTTE - Saint-Benin d'Azy 44
VAUCHELLES-LES-DOMART - Vauchelles-lés-Domart 16
VAULT DE LUGNY - Vault-de-Lugny 55
VIGNE - Ally 61
VILLEMAGNE - Villemagne 87
VILLEMARTIN - Morigny 19
VILLEPREUX - Villepreux 25
VILLIERS-LE-MAHIEU - Villiers-le-Mahieu 26
VIOLET - Peyriac-Minervois 86

WAMIN - Wamin 8
WARGNIES - Wargnies 17

Index of Places

Index of Chateaux with particular facilities

1. CHATEAU RESTAURANTS AWARDED A MICHELIN ROSETTE

***

Reins, Château des Crayères (Restaurant Boyer) 27

*

Carcassone, Domaine d'Auriac 84
Chateauneuf-du-Pape, Hostellerie Château des Fines Roches 113
Divonne-les-Bains, Château de Divonne 67
Eze, Château Eza 100
Eze, Château de la Chèvre d'Or 101
Fère-en-Tardenois, Hostellerie du Château 10
La Malène, Château de la Caze 95
Molitg-les-Bains, Château de Riell 98
Montreuil-sur-Mer, Château de Montreuil 4
Rehainviller, Château d'Adomenil 30
Rochegude, Château de Rochegude 73
Vence, Château du Domaine Saint-Martin 102

2. CHATEAUX WITHIN 50 KM OF AN AUTOROUTE

A1   11 12 13 14 20
A2   1
A4   10 27
A6   18 46 48 50 51 54 55 56 77 78 79
A7   71 72 73 91 92 103 105 106 107 113
A8   100 101 102 109 112
A9   82 91 92 93 113
A10   19
A13   22 23 24 25 26
A15   21
A26   1 2 3 4 6 7 9
A31   36 37 38 39
A35   29
A36   33 39
A40   74
A41   75 80 81
A43   76 80
A48   75
A50   110
A51   104
A52   110
A61   83 84 86 87
A71   58 59 65 66
N1 (Switzerland) 67

3. CHATEAUX WITH PRIVATE SWIMMING-POOL

1 3 11 13 15 18 21 22 29 33 34 35 41 43 46 47 54 56 58 63 65 68 69 71 72 73 74 75 76 78 79 80 81 84 86 88 89 90 91 93 98 99 101 102 103 105 106 107 108 109 112

4. CHATEAUX WITHIN 10 KM OF THE SEA

15 82 93 100 101 111

5. CHATEAUX WITHIN 20 KM OF A GOLF COURSE

3 4 7 13 14 15 18 19 21 22 26 27 44 46 47 48 50 54 56 58 63 67 75 79 80 86 100 101 102 103 109 112

NOTES

POSTSCRIPT

Lecture service
We are happy to give illustrated talks on the châteaux of France to organisations and groups.

Contributions required
Please send us your comments on the château you have visited. The most interesting and informative will be included in the next edition.

Bon voyage.

SYD and ANNA HIGGINS
c/o Roger Lascelles,
Publisher,
47 York Road,
Brentford,
Middlesex,
TW8 0QP.